FAIR
SEAFARER

FAIR
SEAFARER

A Honeymoon Adventure
with the
Merchant Marine

Nancy Allen

Bridge Works Publishing Co.
Bridgehampton, New York

All rights reserved under International and Pan-American Copyright Conventions. Published in the United States by Bridge Works Publishing Company, Bridgehampton, New York. Distributed in the United States by National Book Network, Lanham, Maryland.

Printed in the United States of America

2   4   6   8   10   9   7   5   3   1

First Edition

Library of Congress Cataloging-in-Publication Data

Allen, Nancy, 1937–
Fair seafarer : a honeymoon adventure with the Merchant Marine /
Nancy Allen.
p.   cm.
ISBN 1-882593-20-0
I. Title.
PS3551.L3964F35   1997
813'.54—dc21   97-22081
CIP

Jacket illustration by Eva Auchincloss

Nancy Allen made six voyages on M/V *Endurance* between 1991 and 1996. This story is a composite of those trips. Some of the names, affiliations and circumstances have been changed.

I dedicate this book
to my chief mate

Contents

Foreword

by
Vice Admiral Albert J. Herberger (Ret.)
Maritime Administrator
U.S. Department of Transportation, 1993–1997

"Exactly what is the Merchant Marine?"

Nancy Allen's seafaring husband provided her with the technical answer, but fortunately for us that did not satisfy her curiosity. When she joins her husband aboard the modern American-flag containership M/V *Endurance*, she takes us along on her voyage of discovery. It is an enlightening and enjoyable experience for landlubber and experienced sea hand alike.

The American Merchant Marine consists of the cargo and passenger-carrying ships which are owned by Americans, crewed by Americans, and operated under the American flag according to our laws and regulations. Like Ms. Allen's mate, I, too, had the privilege of sailing aboard the then symbol of U.S. dominance of ocean transportation, the SS *United States*. It is a time fondly remembered, but far removed from today's realities.

I began my career with the Merchant Marine after graduating from the U.S. Merchant Marine Academy in Kings Point, N.Y. I spent most of my seafaring career with the United States

Navy, but the importance of the American Merchant Marine was often on my mind. I saw first hand the unswerving loyalty of our citizen seafarers time and again, in support of America's fighting forces.

Americans were briefly reminded of that proud heritage when President Clinton saluted America's Merchant Marine veterans of World War II during the 50th anniversary observance of D-Day. I was with the president on board the SS *Jeremiah O'Brien*, one of the last Liberty Ships of World War II, and know how much his salute meant to our seafaring veterans.

The heavy losses of merchant ships and merchant mariners during World War II made that conflict the most dramatic for the American Merchant Marine. But its service in support of America's fighting forces was just as important during the Korean, Vietnam, and Persian Gulf conflicts. Whenever asked, our merchant seafarers willingly put themselves in harm's way to serve the nation.

Fortunately, the United States is at peace, and Ms. Allen chronicles the voyage of the *Endurance* as it carries commercial cargoes to and from the United States. Along the way, she shares with us the flavor of shipboard life today. Many of the characters and scenes are colorful, at times inspiring, but she also lets us know the experience can be boring, somewhat dangerous, and at times distasteful.

In the end, she is proud of her ship, of the men and women who sail her to keep U.S. commerce moving, and of the American ingenuity which "invented a better way to transport cargo."

As Maritime Administrator, I share her pride many times

over. American companies continue to be the pioneers in transportation innovation, and American merchant ships have set world standards for efficiency and safety.

And I am grateful President Clinton and a large bipartisan majority in Congress also recognize how important the Merchant Marine is to the United States. The innovative Maritime Security Program is now in place. For the foreseeable future, merchant ships will continue to fly the flag of the United States, and civilian American seafarers will continue to be ready to serve the nation and our armed forces whenever called upon.

To Barbara and Warren Phillips, whose combined talents, insights, teamwork and hard work stitched it all together.

To the seafarers who inspired me with their courage.

And to all of you who:
    read and critiqued the many drafts.
    allowed me to share with others the stories you shared
        with me.
    spoiled me on my shuttles to and from the ship.
    accepted and even encouraged my periods of isolation in
        order to write.
Without your help and support, this book would still be a rough log.

My deep gratitude.

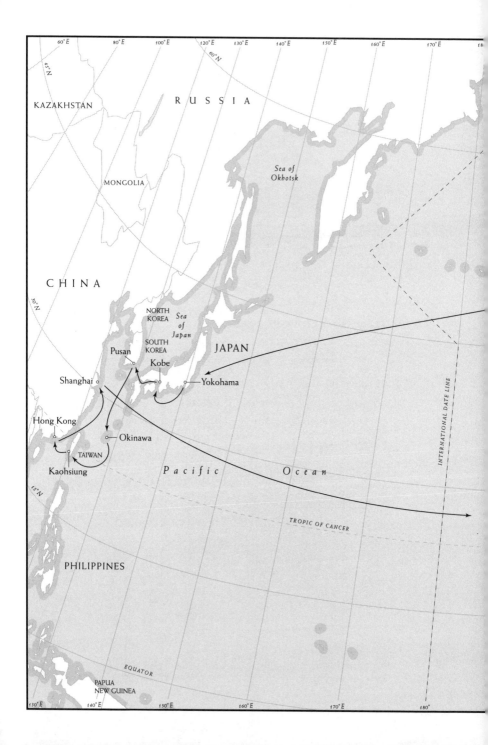

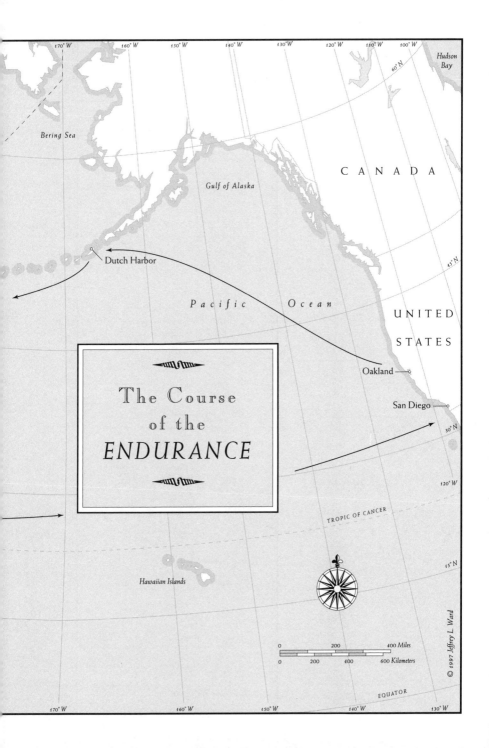

PART I

"A Sailor's Life"

A sailor's life is at best but a mixture of a little good with much evil, and a little pleasure with much pain. The beautiful is linked with the revolting, the sublime with the commonplace, and the solemn with the ludicrous.

Richard Henry Dana

Chapter 1

ABOARD M/V *ENDURANCE*, DOCKED AT SEA-LAND
CONTAINER TERMINAL OAKLAND, CALIFORNIA

NOVEMBER 23, 1994

*It's 2 A.M. as I start this journal. Wait, I have to start thinking like a
sailor: it's 0200 ("zero two hundred" as they say aboard ship) and I'm
writing a log. I can't talk to Bob — he's twitching away in REM. No
sleep for me — this awful racket outside! A few feet from my fifth-story
porthole, a crane operator drops forty-foot containers — those rectangular
boxes you see on trucks and railroad cars — one on top of another. A
puppeteer perched seventy-five feet in the air, the operator controls the
pulleys, his crane, which rolls on a track alongside the ship, and my
sanity. "Crash-crash-crash" . . . then "CLANG," as a steel frame falls and
locks the containers in place, like a Brobdingnagian clamp.*

*This atonal symphony of steel-against-steel has been playing for five
hours straight; now I know why little people commit large crimes. But why
blame the operator? Or even Bob, who warned me this would be no row in
the pond: "Sea-Land has one goal: to get boxes from here to there — fast.
They work the Chief Mate's ass off round the clock. I'll have no time for
you and you might not make any friends — you'll probably be the only*

woman aboard. And by the way, please don't leave your underwear lying around the laundry room . . ."

So here I am on my honeymoon, next to the Chief Mate of the M/V Endurance, a man I barely know. It's maddening to watch him sleep while I cringe with every crash. Mere hours into what I thought would be an Adventure, I'm seriously questioning what I have done. Well, too late now. The containership Endurance is like a big bug caught in a web of docklines and crane wires, and I'm trapped inside.

How did I get here? Actually, this chapter of my life is a short one. Nine months ago, I didn't even know what a containership was. And the U.S. Merchant Marine sounded as strange as the Foreign Legion. I was living in Florida, overwhelmed and depressed. My thirty-two-year marriage had come apart and couldn't be glued back together. Though my therapist certified I was ready to "get on with life," I couldn't find the ON switch. My cat Daphne, my only companion, would even leave her perch by the window to come lie on my chest, as if to say, "I'll protect you."

Then the strangest thing happened. I had an hour to kill between lunch with a girlfriend and the dentist's chair. I stopped at the library and flipped through some boating magazines — sailing was another love I'd lost along the way. I was putting "Cruising World" back on the shelf when it fell open to . . .

POSITIONS WANTED
Trim, tall, youthful skipper (57) retiring
within year seeks sunny, resourceful,
non-smoking lady to help outfit 39' cutter

in Florida. Then cruise Bahamas and
oceans.
Bob Allen . . . (address and phone #)

On a whim, I tossed the page into the copy machine.

A dating-virgin after three decades off the market, I needed
to check the ad out with my buddies. Beth, hardened by
singledom, was not optimistic: "Nancy, for godsake, get real!
What if he's a Ted Bundy?" But Becky thought I should go for
it: "This 50s guy isn't asking for a young cupcake. And he gives
his address and phone number, so he's probably not married."

The only false note was that "lady" thing. I'd rebelled
against private school and the ivy enclave of Brown University
by adding some choice expressions to my vocabulary. It worried Janice too: "He sounds a little old-fashioned; maybe you'd
better start cleaning up your act."

The next day I fired off a short letter: "Hi, Bob, it appears we
have a lot in common. I'm also tall, trim, youthful (53) . . ." I
mentioned that I'd cruised around the Caribbean and would
like to go boating again. It seemed very low-key: Bob Allen
wanted a helpmate; Nancy wanted a sailing companion. No
romance, no commitment.

No commitment? Eight months after meeting this guy, I'd
not only changed my residence, bank and dentist — but my
name. I dutifully filled out a stack of forms, including the ones
Sea-Land required to let me aboard. (It was no sweat to attest
that "Said person is in good health and in all aspects fit to
travel by sea; and further that said person, if female, is not
pregnant" but I had some trouble with "Passenger expressly
assumes all risk of accident and injury to person.")

When Bob's call came, the voice was matter-of-fact, just like the ad. Would I have dinner with him? I'd like that, but could I see the boat first? Sure, it was docked behind his house. I offered to drive up after work the next day.

When I told Beth, she growled, "You're out of your mind! You never *ever* go to someone's *house* on a first date. There'll be little pieces of you floating down the Indian River tomorrow — and I'll have to identify them."

Following Bob's directions and pulling into his driveway, Beth's words didn't seem quite so amusing. There wasn't a cupful of water in sight. I looked hopefully into the sky — no mast. And the car parked out front! What kind of man would own a mud-brown Chevy wagon with bent chrome trim and a crooked bumper sticker inquiring, "HAVE YOU FLOGGED YOUR CREW TODAY?" Ringing the doorbell of the brick cottage in the seaside town just north of mine was one of the most courageous acts of my life.

A big bear of a man with abundant salt-and-pepper hair, Gerard Depardieu with a Roman nose, answered the door. His face had a rosy glow, with hazel eyes and long lashes. A space separated his front teeth, giving him a naughty-little-boy look. Nothing dangerous — just a bit askew like the bumper sticker. I decided to cross the threshold.

Past the pool, across the yard of coconut palms and banana trees, lay the boat, its mast unstepped. We walked down to the double-ender, named *Tusitala*. "Tusitala?" "That's what the Samoans called Robert Louis Stevenson," Bob answered. "It means teller-of-tales." Umm — the guy was a reader. Descending into the cabin though, I wasn't sure what to think. Bob said he'd spent ten years on-and-off building the boat and I sensed from the curved joinerwork what *Tusitala* might become. But picking my way though dangling wires, old cans of paint and resin, rusty power tools, scraps of fiberglass cloth and water-stained manuals, I could see the brown wagon was going to be hauling a lot more epoxy and plywood.

From our table at a nearby restaurant overlooking the Ft. Pierce Inlet, we watched the port side lights of boats gliding in, gleaming like rubies. Over amber ale and blackened tilefish, we checked each other out. Backgrounds OK: his father a language teacher, mine a lawyer. Bob had been a psychologist, I'm an armchair analyst. We were crazy about cats, Benny Goodman and Mozart, "Hagar the Horrible" and film noir. But I had been married forever, it seemed; and Bob, never. It made me sad to hear about the girlfriends who took off when he had to go back to sea. He seemed like such a special guy, surely worth waiting for.

Distant from his parents and two older sisters, Bob turned to solo sailing in a sixteen-foot ketch. It was a natural for him to enter a Merchant Marine academy instead of college, and in the 1950s and 1960s, a young officer could travel the world in style, and make a pile of money. He was able to earn a master's degree in English at Columbia, by shipping out just in the summer months. After he was turned down by med school for being "too old" (36), he got a Ph.D. in psychology and became the chief psychologist of a Halifax hospital. After seven years there, he started to feel as crazy as the patients. That, and the pension credits he'd compiled while in the Merchant Marine, lured him back to sea in the early 1980s.

I look over at the man lying next to me and wonder which layer of his life he's dreaming about.

I didn't hear from Bob for a couple of weeks, and I figured (rightly) he was "processing" other respondents to his ad. Bob would tell me there were forty-one in all: calling, writing, sending cassettes, driving up and flying in. He particularly remembered

- The 23-year-old who wanted to flee from her parents;
- The pretty one — but part of the package was two sullen teenagers;
- The caller who asked him to describe his "equipment";
- The Amazon who could take apart an engine and, he feared, him too.

Finally he cleared them all out, wrote everybody a nice note and got back to me.

However, Bob and Nancy's relationship did not sail briskly along. It felt more like dragging a sea anchor. I was working a double shift at my real estate job. Bob was preoccupied with the sailboat his Applicant was supposed to be working on, hacking into his backyard jungle, and getting ready to ship out with Sea-Land for four and one-half months. We never had time to "date." He would bring Chinese take-out to my house and stay the night. One early morning when the alarm clock rang, he held me hard and whispered, "And I thought I was too old to feel separation anxiety." Then before we could think too much about it, he was gone.

What perversity makes us cherish what — or who — has been taken away? The Chief Mate phoned me from ports in

Japan, Korea, Okinawa, Taiwan and Hong Kong. And he and the ship's radio operator, Josh, cooked up a scheme: Josh used the ship's transmitter to work the ham bands and contact a fellow ham in San Francisco. He would then make a call to me and when I was on the line, patch it back to Josh, who'd wake up Bob. (For his creative and illegal use of *Endurance's* radio transmitter, Josh would be dismissed — a martyr to love.)

Through Bob's letters, I began to glimpse his life out there: "The Pacific is anything but this time of year. Last night there was a terrible roll and I worried about containers going over the side. The steward and cook are fighting; the cook drowns everything in oil. A pair of Chinese junks sailed by at sunset, something you don't see much anymore. And in Yokohama, the Captain and I rode our bikes into Chinatown where we found, of all things, an Australian bar."

I began to learn a new vocabulary. A *terminal* is where the ship pulls in to load and unload. *Reefers* are refrigerated containers. An *AB* is an able-bodied seaman, and the *Captain* (even if young) is *The Old Man*. But best of all, an earthy Chief Mate — the one I hoped was in there somewhere — popped out: "The Chief (Engineer) is acting like a prick." It was encouraging.

Also, the Chief Mate answered my plea: "Exactly what *is* the Merchant Marine?" He wrote back,

"The Merchant Marine is the fleet of cargo-carrying and passenger vessels. (One of my best jobs was on the *SS United States*, manned by civilians. Probably our finest hour was in WW II, before my time; but I did help bring supplies to Vietnam. My ship was anchored at the mouth of the Mekong

River on the eve of the Tet Offensive. There were merchant mariners in the Persian Gulf supplying military cargo for Desert Storm. In the U.S., merchant vessels are regulated by the Coast Guard, who register them, inspect them for safety, license the officers, and issue seamen's documents to the crew. I have mixed feelings about the C.G. because we often get inspectors who seem to work overtime to make our lives miserable."

The crashing of containers over my head doesn't abate. I thrash around in my Procrustean bed. The mattress is too hard, the pillow too thick and my feet are freezing. My resolve to be a good sport is weakening — even with a hero in my bed.

Chapter 2

CONTAINER TERMINAL, OAKLAND

NOVEMBER 23, FIVE MINUTES LATER

I try to rub some warmth into my feet by thinking back to my little bungalow three thousand miles away. I'll never forget the day I moved in — in March, a month after Bob had gone back to sea. My old house had sold and my pen-pal kept pleading for a house-sitter.

It was my first real look around. Off the hallway leading to the bedroom, I stopped in my tracks: a dim room seemed to be bursting with books. I threw my clothes onto a futon inside the doorway, switched on the light and stared at the floor-to-ceiling shelves. Rows of books in Swedish (Bob had spent a year in Stockholm studying drama and blondes); plays, novels and anthologies; everything written by and about Kierkegaard; and a huge psychology section, including one book I immediately began to read — Body Talk.

There were dozens of HOW TOs: *Make Wine, Fly Your Cessna 172, Program in QuickBASIC, Rebuild Your Air-Cooled VW, Landscape the Natural Way.* And, of course, volumes and volumes on sailing: histories, cruising guides, adventures, disasters, designing, building, refitting, engines, electronics, sail repair, knots. It was at that unlikely moment, all alone (even the cat had crawled off), that I really fell in love with Bob.

I pulled out one of the nautical history books; I would need a cram course to keep up with this guy. I never knew that American colonists invented the schooner (a two-masted fore and aft rigged sailboat) or that Yankee workmen crafted the famous clipper ship, so called because it "clipped" days off the regular sailing times. I was awed by stories of wives who'd sailed with their Captains on the clippers. One gave birth during a North Pacific gale, though the crew did reef the topsails for her. Another — all of nineteen years old — nursed her husband who'd come down with brain fever, and navigated his ship for fifty-two days (the First Mate was in irons for insubordination).

These clipper ships of the mid-nineteenth century took long voyages to the West Coast, India and China — at their best, sailing at 18 to 19 knots, almost as fast as Bob's diesel containership. With their long slender lines, tall raked masts and voluminous sails, they enchanted Samuel Eliot Morrison. He rhapsodized, "This harmony of mass, form and color was practiced to the music of dancing winds and brave winds whistling in the rigging. They were our Gothic cathedrals, our Parthenon . . ." John Masefield was similarly impressed:

> Those splendid ships each with her grace, her glory
> Her memory of old song or comrade's story,
> They are grander things than all the art of towns,
> Their tests are tempests, and the sea that drowns

When he came home a few months later, Bob found Daphne, the cat, and me all nested in. We managed some romantic moments, but mostly we *worked*. The garage was like the boat but in triplicate: a minefield of nails and nuts and sawdust pyramids, and an archaeology of Bob's past lives piled into cartons and cabinets. Not to mention the moped in pieces, three dinghies in progress and an old red VW half-hatched into a "Ford Woody." A house that cried for paint; a pool that begged to be backwashed. The jungle out back had re-erupted, a horticultural "Alien."

"Why don't we start with that pepper tree?" Bob suggested. Us two? Take down this monster tree? And we did — limb by limb, branch by branch and finally, root by root. It took a month and a half, in the searing summer sun. I think it was some kind of test because Bob's next idea was, "You know if we cut back the banana trees, they'd make a nice backdrop for a wedding . . ."

Time, in the form of Bob's next voyage, was pressing in again. Company Policy decreed I could go to sea with him only as his Legal Spouse. And so we "got spliced," as sailors say, underneath the pruned trees. The bride and her three attendants wore sarongs and orchid leis; her son Jeff and the bridegroom were attired in Hawaiian shirts and shorts. Beth dressed up her yellow lab as a "flowergirl/ringbearer." Becky read the passage from *Wind in the Willows* about messing-around-in-boats. Janice, who'd helped write the vows, asked us, "Please repeat after me: 'I choose you above all others . . .' " But when the groom came to his part, he ad-libbed, "I choose you above all the other Applicants." We feasted on roast pig, lime-basted chicken, peas and rice, fried plantains and rum punch. Led by the furry flower girl, we danced around the pool in a conga line to "Hot-Hot-Hot."

It took us a week to clean up the mess, try to calm the cat (who knew duffel bags meant trouble) and pack up. In went the new passport and marriage certificate with raised seal. And a copy of *Two Years Before the Mast.* I hadn't read it since adolescence, but its spirit had stayed with me all these years.

I was off to spend two months aft of the mast, in a stateroom rather than the fo'c'sle. But my ship, like Dana's, would be carrying cargo — and a voyager new to the world of shipping, though not exactly a stranger to the sea. I felt many of the same anxieties as Dana: Would I be up to the task? Get seasick? Be accepted? Because he was right: "There is not so helpless and pitiable an object in the world as a landsman beginning a sailor's life."

I reach out to grab Dana and put him under my pillow. He had the courage to climb the rigging and round Cape Horn; I only have to make it across the Pacific. It took him two arduous years to get back home; I'll be on the ship for six weeks and my feet will first touch Alaska in five days, I've been promised. At last, I fall asleep to the loading lullaby.

Chapter 3

STILL AT THE SEA-LAND DOCK

NOVEMBER 24

Thanksgiving Day. My blessings to the crane operators who have the day off. I awake to find the bed empty; Bob said he'd be off early to check cargo. The silence is startling; sunlight assaults my eyelids and peeks into what will be my space for the next couple of months.

Our stateroom (only the Captain has a "cabin") is spartan but surprisingly spacious. The double bed sits in a steel frame with crib-like bars. The night tables, double dresser and bookshelf are done in the same military tan. Two brown Naugahyde chairs, now buried under clothes and duffel bags, attach to the floor with stainless steel chains. I suspect this is not a good omen.

My eyes wander over to an alcove with a mini-fridge on the floor and, dangling from hooks, two life preservers, decorated with whistles and lights; and two orange packets, each labeled SURVIVAL SUIT. How thoughtful: if we go down together, it will be in matching outfits.

A space heater on the floor points toward the bed. Miss November, her photo taped to the wall above it, seems to need it more — for the body parts not covered by her boots and boa.

I note that the TV and VCR on top of the dresser are held down with duct tape and bungee cords; a short-wave radio sits diagonally on one of the night stands. The cord of a wall phone dangles prominently over the headboard. And I can't figure out some strange "decorations": wadded paper towels stuffed in the AC vent, squares of cardboard poking out behind the bureau, and toothpicks stuck in the sides of the mirror.

I get out of bed and drag myself to the head. It's a bare-bones one-person deal: shower, sink and toilet. (Bob once wrote me, mysteriously, "I think of Dorothy's dog every time I take a pee." Ah yes, the Japanese brand TOTO is stamped on the bowl.) Good thing I've left the bubble bath (no tub) and makeup (no shelf) behind. Along with the T-shirts, sweats and jeans I brought, this will surely qualify me as one-of-the-boys. And yet, unless I've dreamt it, there's another female on this ship!

Day before yesterday, the Chief Mate and I stood on the Sea-Land dock in Oakland, watching two tugs elbow *Endurance* in. The size of the ship, a frigid fall wind, trucks squealing up for the offloading, and the acrid smell of diesel were almost overpowering. Still, one corner of my mind was processing the change in the man beside me. The former king of clutter had packed his bag meticulously from a list, checked his watch compulsively ever since we got here (a day early) and dragged us down to the dock two hours before the ship's arrival.

The longshoremen tied up *Endurance* just as you would a small powerboat; except her docklines were the diameter of an arm; and bollards — looking like cast iron bar stools — were used in place of cleats on the pier.

The black hull that loomed above me was unlike any I'd ever seen. But Bob pointed out that this was true form-following-function: "*Endurance's* job is to carry as many containers (we call them "boxes") as fast as possible across the ocean. The pointed bow — see how it turns bulbous near the waterline — pushes through the waves at 21 knots. The deck's flat, like an aircraft carrier, so we can pile on the containers. They're stowed in holds belowdecks too. On one of my smaller break-bulk ships in the 1960s, it might have taken weeks to load the volume of cargo a modern containership can move in *one* day."

I wondered aloud, "How many containers can she hold?"

"Twelve hundred. She was originally designed for 1,000, but the ship was split in half and another section added to gain two extra hatches. They did it in dry-dock: floated the bow section away, then brought in the midsection and attached it to the stern. Finally the front was welded to the midsection. It took thirty-five days and the fit was only ¾″ off at the max. This "jumboizing," as it's called, is common practice on cargo ships; Sea-Land has lengthened all eleven of *Endurance's* sister-ships."

"How long *is* this thing?"

"She's 845 feet — think of almost three football fields — or the length of the *Titanic*. She's over one hundred feet wide and needs thirty-eight feet of water under her keel."

Twenty years earlier, I had sailed to the Virgin Islands with my ex-husband and ten-year-old son. In the shipping lanes, Lykes Line freighters often passed us. Huddled in a chilly cockpit on my night watch, I'd imagine myself warm and dry inside those lighted ships. Now, finally, I would climb inside the "house," aptly named because that's where the crew lives. I counted seven stories of *Endurance*'s house: a square white tower plunked on the deck. The bridge looked like a penthouse with its oversize windows. The smokestack sat behind the bridge like a jaunty cap, displaying the Sea-Land logo — S/L — in black and red.

I struggled up the gangway strung with shoulder bags and cameras. (It would have been tricky, even without the bags, to balance on slanted aluminum "steps" only a few inches in depth — with greasy ropes the only supports.) Then it took five flights of navigating up a narrow enclosed stairway to reach the deck officers' rooms, luggage banging all the way, heart heaving. I had no idea I was in such bad shape.

The Chief Mate threw our bags into the bedroom that adjoins his office. He quickly introduced me to John, the alternate Chief Mate, who was standing there with his bags and an "I'm-outta-here" expression. I could see why John was ready to flee: four people had already formed a line by the desk. And what a strange group it was: a young blond fellow with a high-and-tight haircut, standing military-straight in white cadet's uniform. Then two seamen — one darkly handsome with flowing hair and a dime-size diamond in his ear; the other tall and gaunt, snake tattoos curling out of a Harley T-shirt. Finally, a person about my height (5'9") with short black hair, wearing a green pea jacket, baggy jeans and heavy black boots. Maybe a guy — maybe a gal — I honestly couldn't tell.

So without even changing into his khaki "uniform" (work clothes he buys at Sears), Robert B. Allen became the official Chief Mate of the M/V *Endurance*. The sign-on process is complicated. First the crewmember must fill out a personal information sheet. The C/M checks the sailor's social security number on a Sea-Land list to see if there is a record of citizenship. If not, out comes a federal form and the seaman hands over his passport. (Or it could be a Green Card instead; you don't have to be an American citizen to work on this ship.)

Next is a medical sheet where Joe, the tattooed fellow, was checking off a long "Have You Ever Had" list, beginning with "Appendicitis" and ending with "Venereal Disease." He handed over a letter from his union, proving he'd passed a drug test in the last six months. Then, he filled out an allotment form authorizing Sea-Land to pay out up to 75 percent of his base wage every month. A couple of decades ago, when sign-on was witnessed by a "Shipping Commissioner," allotments could only be made to a wife or savings account (all sailors presumed to be irresponsible). Now more liberal laws permit allotments to a money market account, checking account, or even a girlfriend, provided the seaman writes "sister" on the line requesting "relationship."

Finally, Joe progressed to the final act of the sign-on procedure: the signing of the Articles. The Articles list each crew member's monthly wage and is the legal contract between Master (Captain) and crew, going back to the age of sail. Richard Dana signed Articles when he came aboard the brig *Pilgrim* in 1834; in that era, the document gave the Master permission to abuse his sailors. Today, the Articles weigh in favor of the crew. As one example, if Joe finished signing on, then ran ashore to a doctor, complaining of some symptom, and was able to get an "unfit-for-duty" doctor's certificate, Sea-Land would have to pay his full wages for a voyage he'd never take. This actually occurs, though rarely, to the chagrin of the shipping companies.

The Articles on *Endurance* state that the Master promises "to provide each seaman with at least three meals a day totaling at least 3100 calories, and adequate water, protein, vitamins and minerals." On the other hand, the crew members "agree not to go ashore in foreign ports without permission; nor bring firearms or grog aboard." As I was to find out, "grog" — that festive drink of sugar syrup, rum, lemon peel and nutmeg — isn't the problem. It's the beer, gin, vodka and tequila.

Thanksgiving "dinner" is actually lunch — an indecently early one. Forget holidays, forget Sundays; on Endurance, *breakfast is always served from 0730 to 0830; lunch from 1130 to 1230; and dinner starts at the refined hour of 1700 (five o'clock). So by 12:30 P.M. we're finished with the meal: relishes and rolls, turkey with stuffing, mashed and sweet potatoes, green beans, carrots, pumpkin and apple pies.*

It's perfectly prepared, and all I have to do is line up to be served and after eating, scrape the bones into the garbage — but this "feast" is not what you'd call festive. The five of us at the table eat slowly and say little. I miss my son . . . and the friends who used to bring food, wine, and love. But I promised Bob I'd be "sunny and resourceful." So I try hard to be cheerful.

At least, there are three new men in my life and two of them seem friendly. The Captain is a pleasant surprise, but I've probably read too many stories about murderous masters. No Queeg or Bligh here; he's young for an "Old Man," mid-forties maybe, medium height and very slim. Laugh lines around the eyes and a soft voice. I notice there's no turkey on his plate and he answers before I ask: "I'm pretty much a vegetarian, though I do sometimes eat fish." The Captain is an American married to a Brit; they live in an old stone farmhouse next to Paul and Linda McCartney. I wonder if the couples trade veggie recipes.

On my left is the First Assistant Engineer, who goes by "First." This is just too strange, so I decide to call him Jim. If the Captain looks youthful, this fellow could still be in high school with his round smooth face, Dutch-boy haircut and rimless glasses. He has an eleven-year-old son, who seems to be a computer art prodigy; Jim would rather be with his kid on Thanksgiving too. Across from me is Ed, the Chief Engineer. Because of the system by which containerships are staffed, Bob and Ed are often on Endurance *at the same time.*

The four key officers — those most responsible for the safe and efficient operation of the ship — sit in reserved seats at this single table. Their ranks are Master, Chief Mate, Chief Engineer, and First Assistant Engineer. For continuity and because each officer is guaranteed six months vacation a year, two individuals must be assigned to each rank. These two work out how they will relieve each other. Some officers prefer one-voyage-on/one-voyage-off. Others elect two-voyages-on-two-voyages-off. The C/M has opted for the latter, since he likes the long vacations to work on his projects.

The radio officer, bosun, chief steward and electrician are also permanently assigned, but they don't have an assigned alternate to relieve them when they go on vacation. The resulting "relief jobs" are filled by what is known as "rotary shipping." The other thirteen positions on *Endurance,* from AB to wiper, also come through rotary shipping.

Details differ from union to union, but basically, the seaman who sails rotary reports to his union hall immediately after completing a shipboard assignment. There, he receives a shipping card stamped with the date and time of day. Since every seaman seeking work possesses this card, a theoretical queue-line forms, whereby the value of each seaman's card is determined by how long he has been waiting.

When a seaman wants to go back to work, he begins reporting regularly — usually every day — to his union hall for "job calls." At job call, all available positions, phoned in by a shipping company and posted on a bulletin board, are announced by a dispatcher.

The posting could read like this:
COMPANY: SEA-LAND
SHIP: ENDURANCE
POSITION: WATCH STANDING A.B.
RUN: FAR EAST

The seamen in the hall respond to the dispatcher by calling out the date (or, if the bidding is close, both the date and time) stamped on their shipping cards. The seaman holding the card with the earliest date gets the job, if he wants it. If he doesn't like the run, the pay or the Captain, he may defer bidding until a better job appears.

Rotary shipping, a time-honored method for providing shipboard jobs, can be a hardship. With more candidates than job openings, the sailor often must spend a small fortune travelling to hiring halls far from home. Job hunters who find nothing in New York may be forced to travel to and wait around in such cities as Charleston, New Orleans or San Francisco.

Rotary shipping is meant to be fair to all seamen. Since job calls are public events, dispatchers are discouraged from illegally assigning jobs for payoffs. Yet, irregularities have occurred, at least in the past, and unlicensed seamen have gotten assigned to ships without benefit of open bidding — a practice called "back door shipping."

When the Chief Mate and Ed the Engineer sail together, they kid around, take bike rides and hit the bars. Bob swore to me, "You'll really like this guy." But at Thanksgiving dinner I feel bad vibes. Maybe it's Ed's appearance: thick long hair and beard (Blackbeard comes to mind); pocked skin and under-eye pouches that seem to push his orbs in beyond reach. He's not about to throw me a look or a word at the table. I think of being trapped with him, three meals a day, for the next seven weeks.

I glance over at the other tables for reassurance that I'm OK. A chubby fellow with chipmunk cheeks and a mass of red curls catches my gaze and waves. So does the androgynous one I saw yesterday waiting to sign on. Encased in overalls, "Jess" is "Jessica", the Second Assistant Engineer. Another female aboard. Things are looking up.

The officers' mess is a narrow rectangle with four tables symmetrically spaced along its length. Cadets and visitors to the ship are banished to the farthest table from the Captain's. The next one is reserved for the Second and Third Mates, Second and Third Engineers and the Radio Officer. The table next to the Captain's, unpeopled, is a catch-all for glasses in a brown dishwasher rack; an ice cream scoop in a bucket of water; English muffins, bagels and loaves of bread (raisin, rye, nutty wheat, the spongy white stuff) — all in their original wrappers.

"Centerpieces" on the three dining tables are identical plastic trays full of jam and jelly; catsup and mustard; salt, pepper and Mrs. Dash; soy, Worcestershire, Tabasco and steak sauces. And toothpicks, which are used often and energetically. The tablecloths are supposed to be white linen, but years of food spills and greasy elbows have left some indelible abstractions.

On the inboard side of the room, two shelves hold the coffee pot and toaster, cereal boxes and extra condiments. In a corner sits an industrial stainless fridge/freezer, where you help yourself to fruit yogurt (there's a big rush for this, before it runs out), milk, mayo and ice cream.

Someone has made a small attempt at dining "decor": fake crotons pose stiffly on shelves behind the settees, and plastic ivy pokes out from two planters. Curtains and valances, in wavy shades of beige, frame the portholes. The green walls are bare of artwork; unless you can picture the alarms, bells and switches as pop art.

In spite of the offhand ambiance, musical chairs aren't played in the mess. We're like first-graders, all in our places. I thought the Captain would take the settee seat, which faces out into the room. But no, he's claimed one of the mustard straightback chairs, looking at the wall; while the Chief Mate — and wife — lounge on the settee.

Another old custom keeps the officers separated from the unlicensed crew while eating: the crew has its own mess on the other side of the galley. And yet all stand in the chow line together, first-come, first-served. At dinnertime especially, an outsider could never guess who's who. By that time, the unlicensed have finished their work day (except the ones standing bridge watches); they've showered and put on clean clothes. The engineers who have to go back to the engine room arrive in oily coveralls. The Chief Mate will be working until "twenty-hundred" (8 P.M.) so stays semi-formal in his khakis, but the Captain changes into jeans and a polo shirt after his afternoon workout.

The C/M remembers the way it used to be: the officers wore ties, and a messman in white jacket presented a menu and made recommendations like, "The breast of guinea hen is quite nice today, sir." But those were the days of the "break bulk" ships that carried loose cargo in their holds, lumbered across the ocean and spent days — sometimes weeks — in port. Nowadays, like the ships themselves, the meals have become swift and mechanized.

Chapter 4

STILL IN PORT!

NOVEMBER 25

I'm nosy about the after-Thanksgiving racket outside, so I follow the hallway to a door with a porthole at eye level. It leads out to a stairway that looks down over containers stacked four-high on the main deck, and upward to an empty deck with a railing around it. This seems safe enough. I climb up to find myself nose-to-nose with the vertical strut of a gantry crane overhanging the ship, in the thick of the loading operation.

Six stories below, a line of trucks as tiny as toys run parallel to the dock. They maneuver beneath one of the two cranes working Endurance, wait while their box is lifted up, then lurch off with a diesel fart. It reminds me of planes landing at a busy airport: as soon as the runway is clear, another touchdown.

Just four decades ago, none of this efficiency existed. After Bob joined the Merchant Marine in 1955, he caught a ship to Glasgow, where a dozen longshoremen stood in the hold and stowed scotch case-by-case, as they were lowered into the hold on pallets. Back then, cargo was transferred between dock and ship with booms and winches, slings, nets, hooks, conveyor belts, and small cranes. It's understandable that some of the goods — whiskey in particular — never reached their destination.

One man, Malcolm McLean, who began his career as a gas station operator, is responsible for the revolution in shipping. By the mid-1950s, McLean Trucking had grown from one truck to eighteen hundred pieces of equipment, two thousand employees and thirty-seven truck terminals.

Then McLean made the mental leap of combining flexible trucking with cheap water transportation. In 1954, he bought a freighter and converted it to carry boxcar-size containers. Cargo could now be assembled inland, stuffed into a container, transported by train or truck and quickly loaded aboard converted tankers and freighters. Two years later, McLean's new company, "Sea-Land Service," started operations between New York City and Houston, Texas. By 1966, Sea-Land had moved its first container ship across the Atlantic — from Baltimore to Rotterdam.

Today Sea-Land, the largest U.S. carrier, serves 120 ports in eighty countries. It transports everything from French wine, Dutch beer, Alaskan salmon, German pharmaceuticals and Japanese electronics to American automobiles. Each of its ninety vessels, including *Endurance*, follows a prescribed path — as does most of the world's shipping these days. There are trans-oceanic routes, some using the Panama and Suez Canals. "Coastal routes" can actually include voyages to Alaska, Puerto Rico and even Hawaii. Smaller "feeder ships" generally carry a moderate number of containers to hub seaports. Only the tramp steamers (which have all but disappeared under the

American flag) still travel willy-nilly, delivering their non-containerized cargo to small or out-of-the-way ports.

Despite all this modernization, I'm aware that the U.S. maritime industry is in deep trouble. Sea-Land, APL, formerly American President Lines, Matson and Lykes are the last four major U.S. international shipping companies. According to the U.S. Maritime Administration, only 298 American-flag ocean vessels remain from a fleet that once was larger than 3,500. The number of non-military American sailors has fallen to about twenty thousand from more than 100,000 in 1960, and their average age is fifty years old.

NOVEMBER 25, LATER

A thirty-knot wind is blowing. Containers sway off target; a longshoreman climbs on top a stack of boxes to hand-signal the crane operator. Endurance's departure is already delayed an hour and a half, but trucks are still pulling up to be offloaded. I don't see any order to this madness but suddenly everything stops. Two tugboats, buttressed with tires strung together as bumpers, steam alongside. The tugs pull. The wind pushes. The ship stays cemented to the dock. But with persistence — and 8,000 horsepower — the little tugs that can, do; and we're underway.

Like a pelican, I fly up to my perch on the 06 (sixth level) deck. I grab the rail as Endurance's increasing speed is added to the thrust of the wind. The ship plows past Alcatraz (it looks like an abandoned wasp's nest), then slinks under the Golden Gate Bridge — lipstick-red and rumbling with traffic. As a backdrop, the San Francisco skyline sparkles against a magenta sky slowly filling with stars. The scene needs Beethoven — and eerily, his Sixth thunders over the short wave radio when I run back to the room, hyperventilating from the cold.

The sea has always inspired writers, as a metaphor for the human condition. The thrill of the open ocean combined with danger and hardship for the men who traversed it often brought forth lyricism. Jack London made you feel the fog ". . . like the gray shadow of infinite mystery, brooding over the whirling speck of earth; and men . . . riding their steeds of wood and steel through the heart of the mystery . . ."

But the master of creating poetry from prose was Herman Melville: "There is, one knows not what sweet mystery about this sea, whose gently awful stirrings seem to speak of some hidden soul beneath. . . . Fields of all four continents, the waves should rise and fall, and ebb and flow increasingly; for here, millions of mixed shades and shadows, drowned dreams, somnambulisms, reveries; all that we call lives and souls, lie dreaming, dreaming, still, tossing like slumberers in their beds; the ever-rolling waves but made so by their restlessness."

The headboard phone rings. It's the Captain. "You might want to come up and see the pilot get off; it's going be interesting." I charge up the two flights and grope my way though thick curtains into the darkened wheelhouse. Peering down into a circle of searchlight, I spot a Jacob's ladder dangling between Endurance and the pilot boat. The rope ladder whips back and forth as the little boat is tossed about by waves; the pilot, like a rappeller down a mountain, wobbles and sways in the air, in danger of being dashed against our hull until he's pulled inboard by two crewmen in orange lifejackets.

I feel prickly, knowing my last chance to get off Endurance has passed. Putting out to sea in a storm is not something I've ever done, or would ever do, in a sailboat. I'm experiencing high anxiety — no, to be truthful, it's high fear.

The stories of sailors lost at sea are legend. Ships still founder and sink, crewmen die of hypothermia in the cold winter sea. And we are sailing toward stormy waters, some of the worst after the North Atlantic. On our return, we will sail through a perilous part of the ocean called the Graveyard of the North Pacific.

Lyricism fades and I can only remember Conrad brooding, "The crew of the Narcissus drifted out of sight. I never saw them again. The sea took some, the steamers took others, and the graveyards of the earth will account for the rest."

Yet, mixed in with my fear there's relief (I don't have to navigate or assume responsibility, and I'll be warm and dry if we don't sink) and even exhilaration. The speed and power of this vessel seems rocket-like, and I'm charging out into the unknown. Another seafarer in history's long line, with a man I hardly know and his even more foreign shipmates.

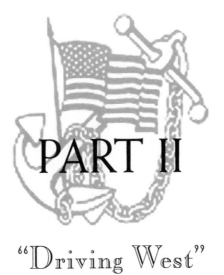

PART II

"Driving West"

One ship drives east and another drives west
With the selfsame winds that blow . . .

Ella Wheeler Wilcox

Chapter 5

CALIFORNIA ASTERN

NOVEMBER 26 0400

Bob assured me, *"The ship's so stable, if I put a glass of water on the night table, it will still be there when we get to Japan."* Oh, right. One lurch launches Coke cans out of the stateroom fridge, opens up dresser drawers (I must have forgotten to slam them until they latched), and bounces an unhooked chair across the room. I sense the wind must have shifted or the ship's changed course. Endurance is swaying like she's heavy in the hips, seas swatting at her stern.

From 2200 to 0315, Bob and his 100-lb. weight advantage roll onto my side every other wave. I'd be on the floor if it weren't for this oversized crib. Along with some sleep, I could use a little reassurance. But the Chief Mate slumbers on, twitching like a contented cat.

When he finally gets up for his watch, I grab all the pillows and build a wall around my body. That's better — but the bedlam! Now I understand the toothpicks behind the mirrors and paper wads: inept weapons against rattles, squeaks and squeals. *"A sailor can sleep anywhere — no sound of wind, water, canvas, rope, wood or iron can keep him awake,"* wrote Mr. Dana. Obviously, I'm not a sailor in his eyes.

Outside, I can hear the containers creaking and moaning from their piled-on weight and wish I didn't know the ship had been sliced in half. I can't help thinking of what happened to Bob, not too far from here:

"About five years ago, I was halfway between Tacoma and Anchorage, on the Alaska run. The weather was awful, with high seas and heavy rolling. It couldn't have been a worse time for one of the containers to cave in — it must have been a defective box because the ones on top of it weren't all that heavy. Thank God no one was on the afterdeck . . . he'd have been squashed like a bug.

"When the bottom box got crushed, the lashings which usually hold everything together loosened up and started a chain reaction. Several containers collapsed onto the deck, nine flew over the side and some hung precariously half over the rail.

"But that wasn't the worst. All of a sudden we heard this menacing *whoosh* and saw flames shoot eighty feet up in the air. Later we realized that one of the crushed containers was filled with hairspray in aerosol cans — and another with rubber tires.

"The entire crew of forty fought the fire for several hours and was able to get it under control before nightfall. But the ship was on old one — built right after World War II — and the containers scraped through the rusted metal deck. Water from the firehoses leaked into the crew quarters and one AB — who stupidly was wearing cowboy boots — slipped and fell. Miraculously, he was the only one injured but he made out OK because he sued Sea-Land. There was no good way to get rid of the water, so we formed a bucket brigade and dumped it down the sinks, where gravity pulled it overboard.

"One other crazy thing: the Captain hove to during the night so as not to lose any more containers, and some supervisor gave him hell for making the ship late."

Well, at least I'm not seasick. Quite the opposite: ever since we put out to sea, I can't get enough to eat. The old adrenaline — the upside of anxiety — must be on overdrive. Bob is amazed by the mounds on my plate: today it was half a roast chicken, oily french fries, zucchini with onions, buttered carrots, a bowl of salad . . . and, oh yes, just a wee piece of coconut cake. He smiled with approval, "The cooks have always fattened me up — it's about time they go to work on you."

The galley is run by a two-person team: the Chief Steward and the Chief Cook. The Steward functions as the Department Head: he makes up menus, requisitions the food, and occasionally cooks and bakes. His budget: $9.76 per person per day. No housewife could do better. (But Sea-Land charges Bob $13.75 a day for me. And I plan to gobble up every penny of it.)

Bob says Endurance has had a strange string of Stewards over the last few years. First there was a fellow whose sexual bent and hormonal swings earned him the nickname "Cinderella." His meals were pinnacles but he needed constant stroking (which no one gets on Endurance), so off he went, without leaving his recipe for banana creme pie. Then they hired a female Steward and everyone got excited about having mother-in-the-kitchen, until she showed a worse temper than Cinderella.

Finally, they found an even-tempered fellow: a white-haired Peruvian whose young wife seemed to drain off any excess testosterone. But Ruben is home in Lima taking care of his wife's needs and his two young progeny, so a substitute Steward has been hired for this trip.

Trying to eat healthily will be a challenge, judging from Steward Louis. An obese belly balloons out from his white cook's jacket, pushing sweat pants down to an indecent level. His mouth seems constructed for strange fare, with a tooth-size gap between incisors and canines. Close-set eyes make you curious about in-breeding. His hair style is oddly eighteenth-century: combed back from the face in a pompadour, waved around the ears, then cascading in shoulder-length curls. Bob laughs. "Here's the scuttlebutt: Endurance has inherited the third Earl of Fopwood."

The Cook, the maritime version of a sous chef, is from New Orleans — where his family owns a small restaurant. John must be at least 6' 5"; his arms drop several inches below his sleeves. He seems quiet and content. He smiles a lot, his large even teeth the focal point of a polished mahogany face.

The Cook and Steward rattle around in a stainless steel domain. The galley is the only place on the ship that looks polished. That is, except for its floor. Even though it's scrubbed down every night, the green tiles alternating with black non-skid squares show age, wear and imbedded oil.

The crew enters the galley from one side, the officers from another — but we all end up in front of the counter together. It's first come, first served, though the good guys stand aside for Bob when they know he has to hustle back to work. The only other times when the crew and officers mingle are at safety meetings and boat drills.

The day's menu — made up on an old AT computer without Spell-Check — is taped to the wall beside the serving counter. Louis and Big John dish out our orders from institutional pots and pans, set in a water bath, which is sometimes hot, sometimes not. Potatoes are pulled from a countertop oven; the carnivores get their meat seared to order on a red-hot grill.

My favorite part of the galley is the salad bar (and Bob's favorite are the desserts on the shelf above it). Bob says the salad bar was installed several years ago — and everyone likes it, even the steak-and-potatoes guys.

After eating, it's back to the galley. I soon get into the routine of throwing silverware into a metal canister on the counter and dishes into a deep sink full of soapy water. Paper and plastic go into a trash compactor, garbage into a plastic bag dangling below a hole in the counter. Endurance practices good ecology by incinerating paper and plastic at sea. Questionable ecology comes with dumping garbage, bottles and cans over the side, even though it's legal to do so twenty-five miles from shore.

I watch the third member of the Steward's Department take over and load up the dishwasher. This poor soul is known in shipboard lingo as the "BR" — which is short for "Bedroom Steward." I see Amin more as a Bolting Rabbit: always in motion, rarely a place to hide, constantly under the gun.

I met Amin the first morning when he came into our room to make the bed and clean up the head. He introduced himself with a bow, welcomed me aboard and asked where I was from. I was more curious about him: this miniature man no taller than my shoulder, with olive skin, black eyes and the friendliest face this side of the Red Sea.

"I'm born in Yemen . . . my wife and four children back there. I come to this country to help my brother in grocery store in Oakland, but too much crime . . . always worry. Much better on ship — only problem: no sleep." I asked Amin to tell me what his days were like:

Alarm rings at 0330; starts work at 0400

0400–0500:	cleans and mops crew mess and officers' mess
0500–0600:	mops passageways on 04 and 05 decks; cleans officers' lounge
0600–0715:	brings supplies from storerooms to galley; sets up for breakfast
0715–0900:	cleans officers' heads and makes their beds (nine in all); changes linens every Thursday
0900–1015:	cleans up after breakfast and gets dishes ready for lunch ("I dunno how many loads go in dishwasher but breakfast more than six.")
1015–1030:	coffee break
1030–1330:	sets up for lunch and cleans up afterward
1330–1600:	odd jobs: cleaning the storeroom and freezer; supplying soap, toilet paper and towels to the "public" heads; counting the hundreds of towels and sheets in the linen locker (*all* the dirty laundry is taken off and done in Long Beach); stripping and waxing floors
1600–1950:	dinnertime set up and clean up; scrubbing down the galley, washing the floor and taking trash down to the garbage room

Running up and down the eight levels separating the main deck and the bridge (no elevator, remember) and along the passageways pared nine pounds off Amin the last voyage. It's a drastic path to weight reduction. He's the lowest paid crewmember at $1340 a month base wage and $7.68 an hour overtime — which, given his hours, he accumulates in spades.

Amin is easygoing, but Bob tells me the previous BR often locked horns with Ruben, his boss. One day the BR shouted to the Peruvian, "You old prick! You think you can satisfy your wife? The minute you leave town, she's with her young stud." I'm learning that the confines of a ship can fray tempers as easily as Endurance cuts into the waves. That got me wondering whether shipboard confines create more outbursts than ashore. I remember Dana making reference to "the differences and quarrels which a long voyage breeds." The C/M's answer:

"It's pretty much the same out here as everywhere else. You get all kinds of people: some fast on the trigger; others passive and slow to anger. I know the times I lose it is when we're in a tight situation, such as docking, and someone isn't moving fast enough or doesn't understand my order. Mostly, though, I realize I'm going to be stuck with the same people for months, so if there's an occasional screw-up, I try to roll with it."

I am also curious about profanity, since "sailors" and "salty language" go together in people's minds. Yet so far on Endurance, everyone's language seems unremarkable. Are they holding back out of consideration for me?

"Not really," the Chief Mate maintains. "What you hear around the dinner table is mostly what you get everywhere else aboard. I may say the f-word a few times more when you're not here, but the worst you'll usually hear is 'sonofabitch.' If you're asking if a female's presence tones down the language, no, I don't think so — at least with the officers.

"Some of the worst profanity I've ever heard aboard ship has come from women. I had a female cadet who was always asking around for skin-flicks; actually, she called them something I won't repeat. And there was a Third Mate who couldn't open her mouth without using a sexual reference. It made the guys on the bridge very uncomfortable, and the Captain went out of his way to avoid her. I don't know whether the women were trying to be 'one of the boys' or were just foul-mouthed in general, but it sure worked against them. It also does a disservice to the females who come on with a professional attitude."

So while the legend of salty sea language still exists, in my experience offensive speech on board Endurance is no more prevalent than it was at Merrill Lynch Realty, where I once worked.

Chapter 6

EIGHT HUNDRED MILES FROM CALIFORNIA

NOVEMBER 27

Gale or no gale, shipboard work continues around the clock. I have to stop feeling sorry for myself when I see what Bob goes through. I don't know what's worse for him: being roused out of bed for his 4 A.M. watch or during rounds after breakfast to check the refrigerated containers. In this weather, it's nothing short of "Reefer Madness."

Most containerships carry a combination of dry, liquid and refrigerated goods. The latter are transported in special containers called "reefers." On *Endurance*, it can be as long as eighteen days before a reefer loaded in California reaches its destination in Hong Kong, so temperature control is critical. Spoiled food means big claims, as high as a quarter-million dollars per container. That's why the Chief Mate — assumed to be the most responsible one, even though he's half-asleep — is stuck with the daily monitoring.

In her two U.S. ports (Long Beach and Oakland), *Endurance* took on 147 reefers. Their temperatures range from $-15°$ (ice cream) to 60° (sugar cane). There's also citrus fruit, meat products, poultry, mullet roe, pork, sauces, yucca, honeydew, celery, beef, beef offal, broccoli, grapes, tomato paste, eggs and lobsters. Sometimes, when reefers are deposited at the container terminal awaiting the ship's arrival, their temperatures aren't monitored during the transition period. By the time the reefers get plugged into the receptacles on the containership, the offal can be truly awful.

Compounding the problem are the reefer boxes themselves — especially those that come into Hong Kong from China, or to Taiwan from the Philippines — which are often defective. They can be suffering from leaks in refrigerant lines, worn out parts that should have been replaced, or low freon. Only a great deal of therapy from the ship's crew can make them behave.

Endurance has fifteen cargo hatches on deck; between several of the hatches stand rows of electrical outlets for the reefers. Most of the reefers and their outlets sit out in the open, where their compressor motors are regularly washed in salt spray. The Chief Mate's task of taking reefer temperatures has eluded the Industrial Revolution: it is done by hand and foot, notebook and pencil. (A system of sensors that transmits temperature data to the cargo's owner in another part of the world is being experimented with. There's a feeling that the bugs in this plan will never be worked out because what ship would welcome a fax that demands, "JUST WHAT ARE YOU DOING ABOUT MY ORANGES THAT ARE READING 70° INSTEAD OF 50° AS MANIFESTED?")

The majority of the reefers are loaded on top of the hatches, located on the main deck. The reefers are loaded directly onto the hatch covers, or on the second tier above the hatch covers. The 220-lb. Chief Mate must access the upper tier of reefers via rusty ladders and catwalks. He worries, "I hope I make it to retirement without falling and cracking my head on the steel deck."

One hatch on the ship — #8 — is dedicated to reefer stowage below deck. A reefer outlet sits alongside each container position, so the entire hatch can be filled with reefers — as many as fifty-two. Carrying reefers belowdecks offers the great advantage of keeping them out of the weather and salt spray.

Determining which reefers need attention is an art as well as a science. You'd think that merely reading the temperature on each dial and checking it against the correct number in the reefer book (which the Chief Mate copies from a computerized manifest) would tell the tale. But the reefers go into defrost several times a day, displaying a false readout (a box supposed to be kept at zero-degrees can read 30° to 50°). Newer reefers have a "defrost" light to signal the cycle, but not the old boxes. If a reefer's been healthy so far, the Chief Mate will assume it's in defrost; if it's been ailing, he'll stick around to see if the temperature returns to normal.

After a couple of hours climbing around this slippery jungle gym on the heaving ship, the Chief Mate goes down to the engine room to leave his list of bad reefers for the Chief Engineer or the electrician. He then stumbles up eight flights to his office, eyes moist with fatigue. At ten o'clock, he's been up for seven hours, after sleeping just five. Only the bitter coffee that's been distilling in the pot since breakfast gets him through the next job: tidying up the reefer book. The temperatures he just jotted down in pencil are now carefully overlaid in ink, ultimately to be photocopied for distribution at the port of discharge. And if they get lost under the piles on his desk or in the copy machine, an emergency is declared.

I'm convinced Bob would sooner misplace his private parts than the reefer book.

After a brief chat with the Captain, at 10:30 A.M. Bob is finally able to take off his shoes and fall on top of the bunk. While he sleeps — a dark dreamless void, he says — George, the electrician, starts wrestling with the reefers.

I'm surprised there's only one electrician aboard. George has an old-fashioned hands-on approach that defies (or transcends) education. Bob says, "Your favorite tablemate Ed is always looking for an excuse to fire George, but I've sailed with a lot of electricians and many don't know a helluva lot about electricity. It's a funny thing with reefers: if you fool around with them long enough, they'll start working. It's like some cancer patients getting better after they've had some TLC.

"I like having George on the ship because he gets out there on short notice whenever I call him. George doesn't need the usual half-hour call-out and I've seen him ignore hurricane-force winds to fix a reefer. Maybe it's his Serbian background: this work ethic. George's other big job is replacing all the light bulbs on the ship. This may sound trivial but when you think of how many thousands there are, and the different kinds, and where they are — all over the place. And he can fix just about anything; I often find

him in the machine shop, welding something together, which most electricians don't do.

"Basically, George is an all-around agreeable, hard-working guy. His only problems will be with you and Jess — the women aboard. George is from the old school: doesn't think females belong on ships. He believes they bring bad luck; he's mentioned that before, when we've had female mates or cadets. I'd keep a low profile if I were you."

Somehow, I don't find George threatening, like Ed the Chief. We've nodded to each other in the chow line and bumped bodies once at the salad bar. The Slavic round face, bald head and stocky body are familiar to me, from growing up in Pittsburgh. And there's something to be said for being taller than your opponent. "Shoulders back, chest out and don't let the bastards grind you down" — that's what my dad used to say.

NOVEMBER 28

The storm has passed and I've been passing out with naps. The earplugs I've borrowed from Jim The First and my vibrating bed now work like magic. The bunk really does shimmy; even though the engine is down in the bowels, it pulsates throughout the ship. I'm beginning to sense when Endurance *slows down from her cruising speed of twenty-one knots (24.15 mph). I can also read the wind direction: when it's astern, we roll; when it's "on the nose," we pitch — just like on my sailboat.*

Finally moving around without fear-of-falling, I decide to start cleaning. It's obvious no woman had ever occupied these quarters; it's definitely time, after eleven years, for someone to dig into the corners. I start in the head with an old toothbrush, wax stripper, and Fantastic. Some of the stains need sandpaper, but the really nasty stuff is now down the drain. Next, I scrape paint and salt off the two 18" x 24" portholes — and now there's a room-with-a-view, or at least half a view. I can see the ocean off to port, but forward it's a sea of containers.

I hope Amin won't be offended; this detail work is no reflection on his abilities, merely his time.

After four hours of labor, the Cleaning Lady has had it. Time for a reward. I've been dying to snoop around the bridge but afraid (1) I'll get in the way or (2) the Captain will throw me out. Still, he did invite me up there once . . . and this is the time he usually works out in the gym. I pull off my grubby sweat suit, scrub down in my sparkly clean shower, and put on proper clothes — fresh jeans and turtleneck — to enter the holiest-of-holies.

Chapter 7

NOVEMBER 28, LATER

Ever since I first felt Endurance's *engine pulsing like a heart, pumping energy through all her systems, I've pictured the bridge as her brain and eyes. Once up there I can see the eyes have a big problem. Because the ship's deck is always piled high with containers — empties as well as the full ones — the Captain can't see the bow or the stern from the bridge. Nor can he spot small boats or navigational aids close by the bow. He has to rely on the Chief and Second Mates to go fore and aft (when entering or leaving port), to report back to the bridge.*

I had a choice of ways to climb to the bridge: either through the same inside stairway connecting all decks or by outside stairs to the bridge-wings: balconies that jut out from the bridge like giant ears. The bridge is a rectangular room eighteen feet deep and fifty feet long, with a front and back section. When I came up at the Captain's invitation that first night, the rear was closed off by thick hunter-green curtains so that lights over the chart table in that section wouldn't destroy the night vision of the men forward, looking out to sea. In the daytime, the curtains are pulled back to make one large space.

The steering station — about the size of a narrow juke box — takes center stage. On its top there's a gyrocompass and below, a puny little steering wheel no bigger than a foot in diameter — including the spokes. (How strange that my forty-foot sailboat had a wheel twice this size). It is yellowish-green steel, the same color as the fiberglass steering stand; I don't think such a homely thing will ever end up on a Lobster Shanty wall.

Gone — along with the varnished wooden wheel of yore — is my concept of a crisply dressed officer standing behind it with steady hand and steely eyes. Bob introduces me to Vince, the AB on his watch. He was the short, dark and handsome one I saw signing on. Vince has replaced his diamond stud earring with a gold hoop. What a pirate he would make with his full beard, long curls and tanned olive skin! Except this pirate is wearing a white golf cap, Hard Rock Cafe Tokyo T-shirt, striped draw-string pants, and Reeboks (heavy on the purple). Also a walloping dose of Eternity cologne.

Vince slouches against the steering stand, his hands in his pockets. Bob responds to my puzzled look: "The AB doesn't touch the wheel unless the ship is docking, undocking or changing course. Endurance spends 90 percent of her time on autopilot or, as we call it, "on-the-mike." Since the GPS system came along, we make more changes than we used to because now we can get almost 100 percent accuracy in maintaining our course. When we encounter strong currents or high winds, I can call out a dozen corrections an hour; but in stable conditions a whole watch (four hours) can go by without a single change in course."

Vince's sloppy posture straightens when Bob calls out from behind the chart table, "Put her on 286, Vince." "Two-eight-six, Mate", the AB confirms, then changes the setting on the gyrocompass connected to the wheel, and ambles over to a blackboard mounted underneath the windows. He bends over and erases the 5 in 285, replacing it with a 6. Since the seas are building again, I suspect his Reeboks will be put to good use sprinting back and forth between steering station and blackboard.

To the left of the steering station is an eight-foot long engine console. The main engine of the modern diesel containership is linked directly to the bridge; the throttle on the console works the same as on a car or airplane — controlling its speed. The ship operates at 27,000 horsepower.

In case the direct throttle control fails, the Captain or Mate can telegraph commands to the engine room by means of a moveable pointer. Eight choices of speed are available, from FULL AHEAD to FULL ASTERN, as well as STOP. This is a version of the old engine room telegraph, found on the earliest steam vessels. And should the electrical system go out, there's a voice-powered phone on the console. It connects with ten different stations on the ship and is operated by a little hand-cranked generator. Its bell "chings" just like an old-fashioned telephone.

Bolted to the floor, to the right of the steering station, is the Captain's perch: a brown Naugahyde barber's chair with gray steel base and pedestal. No one's butt except the Captain's is allowed in this chair. On the other side of the throne three radar consoles stand side-by-side. Two are chest-high electronic marvels called ARPAs (Automatic Radar Plotting Aid), and they allow the officers to track targets much like air traffic controllers. On a corner of the green radar screen, numbers tick off. They record how fast other ships in the area are traveling, what their courses are, and how many minutes/seconds they would take to collide with *Endurance*. The ARPAs are serious business and get a lot of attention from everyone on the bridge, even in good weather.

The small area where the radars stand can be made light-tight by pulling curtains all around — or you can stick your face into a deep plastic hood that fits over each one of the screens. Captain Harvey favors the hoods, and the other Captain who alternates with Harvey on *Endurance* likes the curtains.

On the far right of the bridge, a waist-high counter runs fore and aft. This is where the deck logbook lives. The logbook is an oversize ledger where, once a watch, the Mate records engine revs, course changes, wind (direction and force), visibility, barometer reading, temperature (air/sea), the name of the lookout and helmsman. When docking or undocking, the names of the tugboats. The noon position, taken off the Global Positioning Satellite. A time change, if any. Night orders from the Captain. Inspections/drills/tests (the Chief Mate writes every day — in red pen — COMPLETED INSPECTION OF ALL ACCESSIBLE HAZARDOUS LOADS; ALL SECURE). To a novice, the Remarks section needs some translating: "OCAST, CONT. DRIZZLE. VESSEL ROLLING & PITCHING EASILY IN ROUGH SxW'LY SEA & LONG MOD W'LY SWELL."

The deck logbook is maintained as meticulously as the reefer book. It lets the Mate who is coming on watch see what's been happening. It gives the Captain — whose trips to the bridge are sporadic — an overview. Its entries can be (and have been) used as evidence in insurance claims and accident cases.

I replace the logbook on the counter with proper reverence and then reach for the machine most carefully attended and frequently used on the bridge: the coffeemaker.

The Chief Mate was right about one thing — this "resourceful" business. I'll have to cook up my own amusement. I've been sizing up the crew for potential buddies. It's slim pickings at my table. The Captain is friendly but he is The Master in every sense of the word. How can you get close to someone whose first name can't be spoken? Ed, the Chief Engineer, still fixes his ferret eyes on his plate throughout the meals. Jim-the-First bolts his food and rushes off — either back to the engine room or upstairs to his computer. He says he's fooling around with fractals, which sounds somewhat shady, though I suspect it's something hackers do.

So I've started to stop by the other officers' table with my half-eaten lunch in hand. Some real possibilities here. The rotund fellow with the curly beard — who could be a thirtyish Santa Claus — is Keith, the relief radio operator. He has a trusting shaggy-dog expression and never seems in a hurry. The Second Mate, Frank, looks interesting in a different way: he's a fellow in his fifties whose craggy face suggests he's been around. The Third Mate, I'll probably pass on. Bill is slight and scrawny as a jockey, with the agitated air of a hard-core smoker. On the other hand, Rusty, the Third Assistant Engineer (someone entrusted with the engine named Rusty?) is a bulked-up hunk relaxing back in his chair. And then there's my new buddy, Jess, the Second Assistant Engineer.

I met Jess, formally, in the chow line yesterday. To a tap on my shoulder, I turned around to piercing eyes, inches away. Aquamarine irises flashed at mine like colored searchlights. A black cap of Amelia Earhart hair perched on a square scrubbed face. The voice was deep and direct: "You must be Nancy — I'm Jess." She thrust out an oil-stained hand with blotches on her fingernails and grabbed my elbow with her other one. I can't remember a more intense meeting.

"Uh, hi, Jess . . . it's sure nice to have another woman aboard." As soon as I said it, I wanted to take it back. Jess just laughed. "Yep."

Well whatever Jess was or wasn't, I didn't care — I liked her imme-diately. And she has those remarkable eyes.

I make a promise to visit Jess and Rusty in the engine room (unless Ed bars me from his domain). Keith seems to operate on his own and offers me a private tour of the radio room, located aft of the bridge. "It gets awfully lonely up there in my penthouse," he sighs. He looks like he could use a friend too.

Starting in the early twentieth century, American seamen became increasingly well-compensated for the time they spent at sea, away from home and often lonely. Over the century, collective bargaining has brought higher wages and longer vacations. Neither Jess nor Keith would go back to the old days before World War II when American merchant mariners earned slightly less than comparable factory workers. Now, the differential is more than 200 percent.

Yet these two understand the yin and yang of unionism: corruption versus honesty and dedication; racketeering versus protection for the ordinary worker. Jess is a member of the Marine Engineers Beneficial Association. In July 1995 the former president of its District 1, C.E. "Gene" DeFries, and four other District 1 officials were convicted of transforming their organization into a criminal enterprise that stole more than $2 million from the union and tampering with union election ballots. (These convictions were being appealed as this book went to press.) Yet somehow democracy survives. Rank-and-file members eventually ousted the DeFries group and provided much of the evidence that led to their conviction.

Chapter 8

APPROACHING UNALASKA ISLAND, THE ALEUTIANS

NOVEMBER 29

On the way to breakfast, I spot a postcard thumbtacked to the main deck bulletin board. It says ALASKA WEATHER *above a sketch of the state, partitioned into sections. Coiled isobars, swirling clouds, snowflakes and weather fronts cover the sections with these captions: "Real Shitty, Unbelievably Shitty, Partly Shitty, Intermittently Shitty, Always Shitty, Increasingly Shitty." On a scrap of paper above the card, someone has scrawled "Today's Forecast."*

I noticed something brewing last night when I went up to the bridge after dinner. The change in motion had been barely noticeable, pitching being a kinder, gentler thing than rolling. But in the gray twilight, I saw the bow rising and falling with increasing force, digging white water furrows on the downstroke. By the time Bob got off watch, another growling gale had ambushed us. Endurance *felt like something possessed, with every one of its parts jiggling and rattling. Bouncing around in bed, all I could think of was the god Neptune. I remembered from high school mythology that he loved to pick up ships with his royal hand and bat them around, just for the hell of it.*

Long after Bob had fallen asleep, I lay there, shaken by increasingly sharp jolts — and jealous that the space heater lived on the Chief Mate's side of the bed. When I got up to get another blanket, I felt icy blasts blowing in from the porthole — Zeus, no doubt, joining in the fun. Actually, someone had snaked a cable from the TV set out through the porthole, which left a half-inch crack. I tugged the cable inside, not caring what I was destroying, and tightened the four big "dogs" to squeeze the window tight. It was my only available act of control.

I thought I hadn't slept at all, but Bob's wake-up call on the headboard phone broke into my favorite nightmare: trapped in a French final, after skipping classes all year.

"What time is it? It's pitch black," I groaned.

"0700, the usual," he replied. "Remember we're way up north, around 54° latitude."

"And it's a lot calmer . . . are we out of the storm?"

"Not yet, but we're in the lee of the Aleutians."

The Aleutian chain of islands snakes down in a southwesterly direction from the Alaskan peninsula like a segmented tail, then whips northwest toward Siberia, following the Pacific Rim's tectonic plates. Our forty-ninth state contains sixty or seventy potentially active volcanoes, 10 percent of the world's total, and most of them are in the Aleutians. Fissures, eruptions, and tsunamis are all part of the Alaskan scenery.

The archipelago is made up of about twenty large islands and several hundred smaller ones, stretching a startling 1,200 miles from the point nearest the North American mainland (Unimak Island) to the farthest one out (Attu).

Endurance is heading for one of the bigger islands with the unlikely name of Unalaska ("yoon-alaska"). There, in its port of Dutch Harbor, she'll take part in a modern-day treasure hunt. After previous rushes for fur, gold, copper, and oil, Alaska now attracts sailors of fortune with fish. A convergence of warm and cool currents nurtures seemingly limitless underwater crops, for which the Japanese pay top dollar. Our crew will also procure a bit of this harvest by pitching in fifteen dollars a head for a case of king crab. Bob grumbles as he hands me thirty dollars to take to the Captain (who is arranging it): "I'm not that crazy about crab legs; I hope you can put away more than your share."

The ship steams parallel to treeless brown mounds with ridges raked down their sides like giant claw marks. Behind them, jagged white clumps jut upward like icebergs. These are surges of magmatic rock, thrust up from Mother Earth thousands of feet below. Not a sign of life — no birds or planes overhead, no other boats in the water nor settlements seen ashore. The crew hates even the short stay in port here because the frontier-type town is bleak and little changed from Jack London days. Also, the stop takes Endurance *far north into the succession of blustery gales that spook the region.*

After flat Florida and overpopulated California, this place looks surreal, unworldly to me: the last outpost of the Last Frontier. Still it is land . . . *and strangely comforting after five days of water, water everywhere.*

Suddenly, Endurance *changes course, heading for a pass the radar must be picking up, though it's a mystery to me. Cracking open the bridge door and sticking my head out, I can see nothing ahead but the iceberg shapes, which reminds me that the Titanic was only three feet longer than this vessel. My ears and bronchials feel like they've been injected with ice crystals.*

The sky seems made of folded wool, unraveling with threads of sunlight. Patches of vivid cobalt float over the slate-colored sea like David Hockney swimming pools. Somehow, they make the encircling mountains seem less menacing. I'm surprised by other bits of pigment popping out of the water. I never dreamed I would see a live puffin — that cartoon character that seems a cross between penguin and parrot. Now a whole flotilla of tufted birds floats by serenely, with barely a ruffle of their little yellow plumes. Next, two bald eagles zoom overhead, riding a thermal, then angle their wings to buzz the bridge. As if to say, "Hey, we know the way", they swoop off toward shore.

Now we have other visitors: three tugs have snuggled up alongside, and a Dutch Harbor pilot climbs aboard. If I were depicting the Alaska Man, he would be it. Tall, broad-shouldered, thick dark beard; dressed all in black from wool cap to high rubber boots. Our Marlboro Man of the North maneuvers the ship past Cape Kaleta, Princess Head, Split Top Mountain and Ulatka Head. Skirting past a long sandbar romantically named "Spithead," the pilot calls out orders to the helmsman:

> *Hard to starboard*
> *Dead slow ahead*
> *Slow astern*
> *Stop engines*
> *Dead slow astern*

Endurance inches up to a long narrow dock at the base of a mountain, with the bulk of a lone container crane hovering over it. It's rough, it's wild, but it's still Sea-Land: the crane carries the red and black "S/L" logo.

In 1920, Congress enacted a Merchant Marine Act, popularly called the "Jones Act" after the senator who sponsored it. The law was meant to encourage an American merchant fleet both in commerce and national defense. One of its sections provided:

> No merchandise shall be transported by water, or by land and water, on penalty of forfeiture thereof, between points in the United States, including Districts, Territories, and possessions . . . in any vessel other than built in or documented under the laws of the United States and owned by persons who are citizens of the United States.

In other words, the Jones Act prohibited ships built in foreign countries from carrying cargo and passengers between U.S. ports. Since *Endurance* was constructed in Korea, she cannot transfer cargo between American ports. American-built feeder ships from Seattle have already brought fish from the Pacific Northwest for our pick-up. We will also add containers of Alaskan fish to deliver to the hungry Asians.

As for me, I am, as "Supernumerary," only quasi-crew. American crew members are legal under the Jones Act, but I am not paid crew. Or a passenger, either, which makes my status aboard *Endurance* questionable in Dutch Harbor.

I decide to stay up on the bridge after the ship docks: the best place to watch what's going on anyway. Not much, that I can see. The small town visible from Endurance's *dock is whitewashed by snow; a few frosty blue, beige and rust structures hunker down together, overcome by the mountains. The chart says the big brown bundt cake over to our right, frosted white on top with icing dribbling down its sides, is Mt. Ballyhoo. Halfway up, someone has erected a hand-painted billboard, with a mask-like face mouthing this meditation:*

I Have No Yesterdays
Time Took Them Away
Tomorrow May Not Be
But I Have Today

My eyes pan right — attracted by an eagle perched like a gargoyle on a dockside dumpster. It feels like I'm part of a David Lynch production.

When I figure it's safe to come out, I tiptoe back to Bob's office, where I find Jess waiting for me. "Heard about your little problem with Immigration," she says. "Ready to go ashore? Grab your jacket and I'll run interference." The daredevil in Jess spirits me down the outside stairway, then pushes me into the electrician's room while she checks out the gangway for "uniforms."

All clear, we set off down an unpaved road leading into town. Such glamour we have: me in my XL thrift-shop parka and Jess in her camouflage jacket and matching cap with the ear flaps down. Just as we get abreast of a narrow airport runway, a Blazer (its factory color a mystery under several layers of snow and dirt) pulls up. A woman in her thirties with a mop of dark curls and a pale round face made serious by glasses calls out the window, "Hey! Can I give you a lift?" Jess turns to me and says, "I wanna check out the airport, but you go, and I'll meet you at the Elbow Room in a couple of hours." (Ship's scuttlebutt has it that "Playboy" rated The Elbow Room the "Third Meanest Bar in the World." Jim the First offered to bring me some lube oil to dab behind the ears so I'd smell good to the fishermen.)

I'm happy to hitch a ride because the foot of ice on the road has already frozen my feet through two pairs of wool socks and boots; and my turtleneck, wool sweater and cheap parka are no match for the gale force wind. "I'm Anita; are you the Chief Mate's wife?" the one at the wheel asks. She laughs at my surprise: "I heard you were coming out this voyage; I work for Marine Operations; we handle the ships and hear all the news. I made some time to show you around but I need to stop by the office first."

Anita and her two co-workers — no-nonsense women wearing sweat-suits and work boots — share one large room in an obviously new building. It's spare of furniture and carpet chemicals sting the nose. Huge windows frame two scenes: the harbor and the airport runway. Anita points to a prop plane wobbling toward touchdown. "If we want to get out of here, we have to fly. I hate it. There's no control tower. The pilots have to find their way over one mountain range — usually buried in clouds — and slam on the brakes before hitting the next one. The runway's so short, the road I picked you up on gets closed off, to give the pilots a few extra feet. The last time I landed, there were hurricane-force winds. I'm ashamed to admit I cried from fear the whole time we were crabbing down.

"Before we go, I have to call over to Endurance. They're mad because I had them move fourteen feet forward, to work the cargo. (I chuckle at the image of tiny Anita, five feet probably in her boots, directing the 845-foot ship.) But if they bitch too hard, I won't deliver the toilet paper someone in California forgot to put aboard."

Back in the Blazer, Anita drives fast and fearlessly to her house along an icy, treacherous road. She talks non-stop. "Have you been to Australia or Costa Rica? We're always looking for a warm spot to vacation," and then, "I do love it here. The natural beauty is awesome. But there's one big problem: the transient population. I used to get close to people, and then they'd move away. It's sad, but now I've learned to keep my distance. I still have two wonderful pals who befriended me when I came here from Bristol Bay. I don't know what I'd do without them.

"I can't believe how Unalaska has changed since I arrived in 1983 with my first husband. Everything was old and falling apart. If a couple needed to expand their place, they'd find an old wreck of a hut left over from World War II and throw it up alongside. Now we have a $250-a-night hotel (the same room would cost a third of that in Seattle), a sports complex with an indoor track, and a big new clinic. I'll never forget getting an X-ray in the old one . . . walking past a bunch of stinky fishermen, dressed in one of those half-open hospital gowns.

"Here's the Eagle Supermarket; when one of their containers arrive, it gets the royal treatment. And there's the Holy Ascension Cathedral, from 1825, the oldest Russian church in Alaska. The Russians were after furs; a single otter skin could bring three times their annual income back home! See that pair who look like Eskimos? They're Aleuts (Anita pronounced it "alley-oots"), the tribe that crossed land bridges from Asia thousands of years ago. They still have a settlement in Unalaska. They named Alaska: it's Aleut for 'shores where the sea breaks its back.' Over there is one of our fish-processing plants, which is what drives the economy here: there's over forty thousand crab pots in the Bering Sea at any given time and hundreds of boats emptying them. We're finally starting to attract tourists — especially Germans — who love to go tramping around in the wilderness."

Some Higher Power guides us up the slick winding road to Anita's house on a nearby mountain. The roads, narrowed by snowdrifts, glisten with ice (the storm that slammed Endurance around yesterday also dropped three feet of snow on Unalaska). Anita is careful to park facing into the wind, explaining, "I know people who've had their car door ripped off by a gust." She steps out nonchalantly in her silver ski pants and quilted jacket, not even bothering to pull up its hood.

Anita's A-frame, painted a muted blue, is glued to the mountainside by some miracle known only to the builder. From her floor-to-ceiling windows, we just make out Endurance, a speck in the distance. Contrasted with the windy whiteness outside, the living room seems almost tropical: live plants hanging, two parakeets chirping, a well-fed cat sleeping off its last meal. A pot-bellied stove blows heat into the tall narrow room; rows of CDs,

videotapes, and books are ready to warm the soul, and stylized images of
boats and birds splash color onto the walls.

Proud of her feathered aerie, Anita announces, "Follow me — I've saved
the best for last." She opens the back door and sidesteps down a snowy
incline. Fearing a flight into oblivion, I slide down on my fanny. Anita
leads me into a framed-in sunroom she and her new husband, a carpenter,
are adding on. "We've planned it to catch every single ray. And we're
putting hot-water heat under the floor. See, there's my early Christmas
present." She points to a leather tool belt dangling from a hook. At first,
Anita had seemed an unlikely Alaska Woman, with her studious face and
slight frame, but the tool belt is a symbol of the strength that enables her to
survive, even flourish, in this harsh place. She has become like the puffin,
unruffled by the cold.

Much as I hate to go outside again, it's nearing the time I'm supposed to
meet Jess. In the car, Anita apologizes, "I'd like to take you up to see the war
bunkers, but the roads . . ." "That's okay", I interrupt. "Sea level will suit
me just fine. You can tell me about it." And she does.

During World War II, the Aleutians were in a strategic place. If
the Japanese took Alaska, they'd have been within bombing
range of the Boeing plant in Seattle. Russia too. But even after
Pearl Harbor, the U.S. War Department pretty much ignored
Alaska. It got some old World War I destroyers and a few army
garrisons and airfields throughout the islands. Dutch Harbor
became a Naval Air Station.

In 1942, the Japanese set out to attack the Aleutians, partly
to set up a beachhead but also to divert attention away from
their main target: Midway. On June 2, they steamed toward
Dutch Harbor with two heavy cruisers, three destroyers, and
two aircraft carriers, supporting more than eighty planes.

Their plan was to bomb the base while their troops were landing on Kiska and Attu.

As usual, the weather was bad. A cold front and heavy fog. But during a brief break in the clouds, a U.S. patrol plane — a PBY flying boat — spotted the ships. When Japanese airplanes started dropping bombs early the next morning, anti-aircraft guns were ready. And the climate actually "cooperated" because most of the enemy planes lost their bearings in the fog and had to turn around.

It took a year for the U.S. to get Kiska and Attu back. Though there wasn't much action in the Aleutians until the battle for Attu, it was crucial, psychologically, to reclaim them because they were the only spots in North America where the Japanese got a toehold. Again, fogs and gales played a huge role: both countries came to realize *they* were the real enemy. Meanwhile, the Japanese were diverted from Midway by their campaign in the Aleutians, so the Americans were able to hold the island. Many people think these events turned the tide of the war.

With a promise to visit me in Florida and bake in the sun, Anita drops me off at the Elbow Room. Cautiously, I open the rough wood door, expecting a dark room lit only by the glint of knives. Instead, pale light shines through dirty windows into a narrow room divided into thirds: red-upholstered booths, the bar area and a dance floor with a deluxe drum set taking up a corner under silver tinsel strung overhead.

Jess and Keith are sitting at a round table a few feet from the bar, on high stools with shedding stuffing. Keith wears the blissful face brought on by high blood alcohol level; Jess' intense look has softened somewhat. "I'm having another White Russian and a bowl of popcorn," she says with a smile. "What can I get ya?"

I sip a plastic cup of stale burgundy and look around. A middle-aged couple in parkas sit chain-smoking at the bar, looking as vacant as Manet's absinthe drinkers. A ponytailed father is showing his preschool kid a disposable Kodak camera. Behind the bar are lighted ads for Bud Dry and Alaska Ale and a reclining nude in a gilt frame. Lusciously-painted, she probably saw better days in a boomtown brothel. A photo of Jimmy Buffett and his seaplane hangs in a corner; he once played a gig here. Incongruously, a shelf full of bowling trophies decorates the adjacent wall.

The two barmaids won't be mistaken for twins. The short middle-aged Aleut wears tight black curls and over her left ear, a plastic purple flower — the color of her short ruffled dress. The tall pretty one has done her hair in a French braid; she looks classy even in jeans and a plaid shirt. I ask, "What is your accent . . . Scottish?" "Yes, I followed some friends over six years ago." "And how do you like living here?" I probe. "It suits me fine."

I think about this: sky-is-the-limit types emigrating to a bleak, gale-driven sliver of tundra in search of adventure, money or escape from who-knows-what? For Jack London it was all three and he said in The Sea Wolf "Dutch was a boom town and looked it."

Jess and I leave Keith — with a fresh pitcher of beer — at the bar. "You go on," he tells us. "I'll get a cab later." We trudge back silently to the ship, our throats automatically sealed against the wind. It gives me time for more reflection on the women I'd met in the last few hours. They seem to share a pioneer-type hardiness, which I see in Jess too. What's the matter with me? Though I marvel at nature in the buff, I also can picture the mud and dirt when the snow melts. I know there is lavish life underwater but no way would I plunge my bones into it, even with the most high-tech wetsuit.

People who enter your life only to suddenly depart; wind and fog that won't go away . . . not my style.

No, if I had to live here, I'd probably hang out in the Elbow Room and drink away the days until the midnight sun reappeared. The burgundy has done its job: my insides glow and what little color I spy on the way back — a blue shutter, a black truck — looks sharper and brighter.

Endurance leaves Dutch Harbor several hours later with 218 more reefers. They are full of frozen cod and cod roe, salmon, surimi and "opilio." ("Sounds like an immoral act," the Chief Mate comments; but I think it's a type of crab). Among them a dozen mysterious reefers containing "Subsistence" and "Cat Vegetables." Appropriate products, perhaps, for the Inscrutable Orient. We are heading for Yokohama.

Chapter 9

NEAR ATTU AT THE END OF THE ALEUTIANS

DECEMBER 2

This is a day to remember because we lost yesterday. There simply was no Dec. 1, because Endurance *crossed the International Dateline. Such an event should have serious existential significance, demanding reflection on my part. I ask Bob, "If I'm really bad today, which I guess is yesterday — or is it tomorrow — does it mean I get away with it?" He shakes his head, "Sorry, my dear, that's not the way it works. When we cross the dateline homeward bound, you get the day back again, plus another one. So you'd be punished twice."*

On the bridge, a marine quartz clock allows you, with the press of a button, to advance or retard every clock on the ship by twenty minutes. We're adding one hour to each day now; the three Mates share the time change on their night watches. Bob lifts my finger to the button and intones, "This is as close to God as you're ever going to get . . . tampering with time."

The Captain and Chief Mate peer at the computer monitor. It shimmers with brilliant blue, green, orange and red ellipses. Without thinking, "WOW!" pops out of my mouth. Bob frowns at me but when the Captain *turns around, he's smiling. "I'll bet you haven't seen this before, Nancy. I just called the satellite system — to the tune of $28 — downloaded the information, and what you see on the screen are wave heights for the whole Pacific.*

"I wish we were in one of these nice blue or green spots but we've gotten ourselves into an orange. The two reds are the last-of-the-season typhoons: we've already skirted YURI, but now ZELDA is bearing down on us. Say Bob, let's head north a bit . . . and slow her down to 17 . . . we'll see if we can make it a bit more comfortable for breakfast."

That's what they pay the Captain $140,000 a year for. It's true: he doesn't spend much time on the bridge but when he's there, he's in total control. He analyzes . . . he orders . . . the ship and its cargo arrive intact and on time. Captains, like Harvey, who are soft-spoken and consistently think about the crew's comfort — like finding a calmer course at mealtime — are a minority. Too often, according to scuttlebutt, they haven't evolved beyond Dana's Captain Thompson whose "unlimited power upon long voyages takes away the responsibility, and too often, even in men well disposed, gives growth to a disregard for the rights and feelings of others."

Some things never change. This is still the code on cargo vessels, as true now as it was for Dana: "The Captain is lord paramount. He stands no watch, comes and goes as he pleases, is accountable to no one, and must be obeyed in everything, without a question even from his chief officer." However, there's a story which illustrates the perils of command.

The Captain of one cargo vessel, operated by another shipping line, decided to take some vacation time. His company got a relief Captain for that voyage: one of their Chief Mates. Though this C/M had experience on the same type ship, he had never been on that particular vessel or route before.

Most Chief Mates hold Captain's licenses, and many will indeed move up to a Captain's position. But in the shipping industry, a lot depends on who you know and what school you attended. Alumni from each of the six U.S. merchant marine academies are excessively loyal to each other. So a graduate of the Kings Point Merchant Marine Academy, working for that shipping company in an administrative position, was able to place his schoolmate, whom we call C/M Golden for the purposes of this story, in the opening for a relief Captain.

Once aboard, Chief Mate — now Captain — Golden was congenial to the officers and cordial to the crew. It looked as if he had the Right Stuff to work up to a permanent Captain's position with his own ship.

And then it happened. His ship anchored overnight outside Pusan, Korea. This is a burgeoning port with too little dock space; often ships must anchor, or drift, and wait for a vacant slip. The next morning Captain Golden weighed anchor and headed for his slot in Pusan Harbor. It was clear and calm.

The Chief Mate on that vessel, with his walkie-talkie, was at his regular station on the bow. The Bosun was standing next to him. The C/M watched with increasing concern as the ship headed toward a huge rock, really a 170-foot pinnacle, jutting out of the water near the harbor entrance.

As the ship's Chief Mate later told the story, "We always

keep to the south of this rock when shifting from the dock to the anchorage. I figured the Captain must have checked the chart and found the rock steep-to (like a vertical wall below the surface). It is *never* good form to second-guess a Captain, but I had this really sick feeling, and then the ship shuddered. Knocked the Bosun right off his feet!

"So I got on the walkie-talkie: 'Uh, Captain, I do believe we hit something.' There was a long, long silence. Then he came back, 'You know, I think that was a heavy swell from the north.'

"After we tied up, I ran to the bridge and pulled out the chart. There was a 24-foot shoal leading out from the rock where we had grounded. By that time, Golden had changed his story and maintained the keel had struck 'an unidentified submerged object.' When divers went down, they found a 140-foot gash in the bottom which had sliced into two ballast tanks. If they had been fuel tanks, you'd have heard about the spill on the news. So we offloaded all our cargo and headed for the nearest dry-dock, in Nagasaki. Four weeks and $1.8 million later, the vessel was back in service. Captain Golden was relieved in Nagasaki by one of the regular captains and returned to his Chief Mate's job."

Bob and others who heard the story tell it over and over. Captain Harvey can't get enough of it: with his years of master's experience he never would have gotten boxed in; if he found himself in trouble, he'd have skillfully maneuvered his ship out of danger. The stern of a single-screw ship, even a huge containership, tends to swing to port when backing up. This also makes the bow pivot to starboard, exactly what was required at that critical moment.

Captain Harvey and his Chief Mate speculate endlessly. Was Golden too stubborn to take evasive action? Did he neglect to study the chart? Or misinterpret it? Did he freeze? Or was there some other explanation?

Meanwhile, Endurance's chart of Pusan Harbor has been updated. "Golden Rock" is scrawled in red ink over the rock's official name "Saeng Do."

DECEMBER 2, LATER

After teasing us with hot-tempered winds, muddled seas and capricious courses, Typhoon ZELDA makes her move. Less than two hundred miles away, she attacks Endurance with bursts of rain and a "high confused swell" (so says the logbook). I'm spending a lot of nervous hours on the bridge; Captain Harvey is always there. He paces a continuous loop from the windows to the radars to the chart table to the barograph. In eight hours, the needle has fallen almost vertically: from 1028 to 991.2 millibars. That rapid drop in pressure means we're in for high winds and seas — a whole lot of trouble.

Was I being paranoid? Why did we see a video on hypothermia today? *Endurance* has a library of training films, and viewing one of these alternates with "hands on" fire and boat drills. This week's video was a Coast Guard production. The U.S. Coast Guard now requires that all vessels navigating northern waters carry survival suits for all crew members. The film teaches that the main danger of falling into these frigid waters is hypothermia: subnormal body temperature that can kill in minutes. So these $450 outfits not only keep one visible (they're bright International Orange) and afloat, but they also encase the wearer head-to-toe in insulated material. There is one little rectangle for eyes and nostrils.

Afterwards, we were ordered to go try them on. The preferred technique is to lay the thing out on the floor and wiggle into it while prone. My struggle with the built-in boots and mittens and hood and zippers and Velcro looked like nothing in the film. Fortunately, my dress rehearsal was performed without an audience. Since, according to the film, "One Size Fits All," I'd have given anything to see the performance of Big John the cook.

DECEMBER 3

The sounds in the room are progressive jazz. The engine, like a kettle drum, beats out the underlying rhythm. Superimposed are violin-like screeches and odd bursts of percussion. Outside the porthole the wind instruments tune up.

I wedged myself in bed most of yesterday, reading Nelson DeMille's Gold Coast. *The manicured estates of Long Island seemed a planet away from this jerky hunk of steel. I made sure all the chairs were hooked to the floor, then tied the refrigerator door with rope and double-checked the drawer catches. The only thing I forgot was the short wave radio, and ultimately it bounced off the nightstand onto my forehead. So I'm wearing a purplish egg over the eyebrow, a badge of typhoon oversight.*

I stagger down to breakfast. We have to hold onto our plates because the tables aren't gimbaled — that is, rigged to remain horizontal when the ship tilts. The Captain announces that during the night, the wind gusted over 60 knots and the ship listed 26°. I confess, "A couple of times there, Captain, it

felt like we weren't going to round up. I was literally holding my breath.
Tell me honestly, were you worried?"

Captain Harvey answers in his soft calming voice, "Well, any time we
have that kind of rolling, there's a real chance of losing containers. But I
wasn't concerned about the ship itself — she's been through much worse."
He tells me about one of those times.

In March of 1984, *Endurance* — pretty close to our current
position — was caught in a weather system that brewed up
without warning. Sailors used to call these things "Pacific
bombs"; meteorologists now tag them "explosive lows." There
was no time to get away from the storm; basically it boiled
down to survival.

For several hours, *Endurance* battled Force 11 and 12 winds,
with gusts over 95 knots. The seas built to forty feet. And then
a rogue wave — over 100 feet high — bore down on the ship.
Captain Harvey watched in horror as it crested directly over
the bridge.

Good old *Endurance* rolled over 46°, hung there, and then
ever so slowly righted herself. Amazingly, there were no serious injuries and just two containers were swept overboard.
But one of them was full of Sony stereos worth a half-million.
Sony's insurance company paid off, then sued Sea-Land, trying to prove negligence. Captain Harvey flew from England
for three days of court testimony. He said that all he needed to
exonerate himself and Sea-Land was to tell the truth and
produce the logbook and barograph chart.

The judge ruled that no one was at fault: the loss was simply
a "peril-of-the-sea." This concept, originated by Hanseatic

merchants and ship owners, has formed a cornerstone of admiralty law. Since you don't hear much about that defense these days, the case was written up in the Federal Register. And Sony still ships with Sea-Land.

"Is that story supposed to reassure me?" I question the Captain.

LATER

ZELDA has stormed off with a few parting tantrums. Because of the rough weather, Bob has kept an eye on Ken during Reefer Madness, while showing him the ropes. Today, the cadet will get his feet wet — literally.

Bob lays out the rainy-day routine: Ken will dictate the reefer temperatures into a tape recorder tucked inside a waterproof bag, as the rain would turn the reefer book to pulp. When he's through and back inside, he'll play the tape, and enter the figures — in pencil first, please, then ink — in the book. I can see that Ken is petrified; he doesn't say a word. Bob ends his lecture with, "Think of this reefer log as the family Bible. I don't want you to smudge it, smear it, or fold it back because the cover will fall off. And if you lose it . . ." He doesn't have to finish. Ken is turning white.

Ken seems out of place on this working ship. Even though he's put away the starched whites he arrived in, his new navy blue coveralls look pressed, and his work boots are right out of the box. His blond buzz-cut, smooth skin, straight teeth and military posture seem a tribute to genetic engineering. Unlike the drained faces in the chow line, Ken's is bright and eager. He shows up early every day, with a pad to take notes. The Chief Mate is "Sir"; the Chief Mate's spouse, "Ma'am."

Ken fell into the Merchant Marine this way. "Well, Ma'am,

even though I live way up in Wisconsin, my uncle's a Mississippi River pilot, and he got me interested." Ken is now a sophomore at the U.S. Merchant Marine Academy at Kings Point, Long Island. The other five academies (in Maine, Massachusetts, New York, Texas and California) are state institutions; King's Point is the only one run by the federal government. Ken needed a congressional nomination, just as in the military schools. After graduation, he'll have to give the government five years' service in a marine industry but meanwhile, his outlay for incidental expenses is only about $1,000 a year. As part of his degree requirements, Ken must spend 300 days at sea on several different ships; this stint on *Endurance* is his first time out.

Most cadets choose either a deck or engine curriculum but Ken has signed on as a "dualie," which means he'll spend half the time with the deck department and the other half in the engine room. (Dual training is becoming a popular option for Kings Pointers. The theory is that a dualie could go down and fix the engine before standing watch on the bridge.) After a total of four years, Ken will graduate with a B.S. degree and both a Third Mate's and Third Engineer's license.

I question Ken some more after he and the reefer book return intact: "So tell me, what's the good and bad news about Kings Point?"

"Ma'am, we have a 40-foot sailboat run by the midshipmen. I can go out in it every day — I don't think that'd be the case at Annapolis. But we all hate the food: 'chicken parts' are really chicken strings. I'm a wrestler and need to watch what I eat; that's not easy on institutional food. Actually, some higher-up told the cook we should be eating less fat, so he started leaving the cheese off the cheeseburgers, but some of the cadets staged a walkout.

"*The biggest problem, really, has to do with choosing a Merchant Marine academy over a regular college or university. No one seems to know what the Merchant Marine is all about. I dated someone who said, 'You're going with the merchant marines? Aren't they the guys who run guns to Central America?'* "

I hate to admit I didn't know much more about the Merchant Marine than the girl Ken dated. But now I'm motivated enough to dig into the past. As the Officer's Library has been taken over by videotapes, I ask Bob if there's another library aboard. "Down on the 03 deck. You'll have to turn right and go past the crew's gym, so don't be shocked if you see someone in his skivvies."

I run past the gym door into a room about the size of a walk-in closet with two walls of overflowing bookshelves and cartons of magazines and paperbacks strewn about the floor. It's like a stall in the flea market, but all mine.

There are hard covers, soft covers, and no covers; some waterlogged, some underlined and many never-opened. As I might have guessed, the adventure and suspense writers reign: Stephen King, Tony Hillerman, Elmore Leonard, John D. MacDonald, Dick Francis, Tom Clancy. But like finding a Liz Claiborne blouse in a bin of T-shirts, I dig out Joyce Carol Oates, Edith Wharton and intriguing titles like Bastard Out of Carolina. *I also find, between Dr. Spock and* The New Testament, *an* Atlas of Maritime History. *I sit down on the floor and start reading. Not too bad. The authors are humble; they admit that no one knows when merchant shipping began.*

By 1500 B.C., Egypt, Crete, Greece and Phoenicia were building ships with long keels, able to survive the open sea. Then the Greeks began trading among their colonies (scattered around Italy, France, North Africa, and the Black Sea).

Archeologists continue to unearth their amphorae — the enormous clay jars which were that era's "containers," stored as they were in warehouses, then carried aboard ship. When Rome became a super-power, her galleys traded throughout the Empire and indulged her citizens back home with exotic foods and luxuries. (*Endurance* still follows this pattern by delivering Japanese cameras to Hong Kong and embroidered sweaters from Hong Kong to American boutiques.)

Next came the Viking explorers, Hanseatic merchants, Crusaders, and the Italian merchants who dominated the Middle Ages. The rudder was invented then; nautical charts were drawn up; and the compass found its way from China to the Mediterranean.

And the Age of Exploration: Portugal, Spain, England, France and the Netherlands, all building ships and looking for India. Also, the shameful era of the triangular slave trade whose three legs transported rum and iron from America to Africa; slaves, gold and pepper from Africa to the West Indies where the slave ships added sugar, molasses and mahogany; and proceeded to America again. The founder of my alma mater, John Nicholas Brown, came from one of the mercantile dynasties whose wealth was tainted with slaves' blood.

So ends Part One of my history lesson. When I look in the book's index under "United States," I find six entries for the Marines and eighteen for the Navy. Zip for the Merchant Marine. I see Ken's point about this secret service. I'll have to do some more digging.

Chapter 10

DECEMBER 4

My hero, R. H. D., wrote, "No man can be a sailor, or know what sailors are, unless he has lived in the forecastle. You hear sailors' talk, learn their ways, their peculiarities of feeling as well as speaking and acting; and moreover, pick up a great deal of curious and useful information in seamanship, ship's customs, foreign countries, etc., from their long yarns and equally long disputes . . ."

My female friends have asked me to put down all the lurid details of life on the ship. Well, Dear Diary — and Beth, Janice and Becky — if I were to write about "Shipboard Sex" from my personal experience, it would be a very short chapter. The Chief Mate is overworked by the company, not me; I can't say I wasn't warned. However, I do have something of a scandal to report.

This morning at coffee break, the Captain hands me an old fax. It's an article from the front page of the Journal of Commerce, *dated November 20, 1991, and titled "Women Ship Employees Cite Sexual Harassment on the High Seas." My mouth opens when I discover the locale of the story — right here aboard* Endurance!

It seems that one Laura K., a licensed ship officer and Desert Storm veteran, was the Third Mate on Endurance *a few months earlier. Laura was not pleased that* Sports Illustrated *pictures of models with sparse swimsuits and notable nipples were taped up in the workout room; and photos of women in only half their suits graced the slop chest (a kind of company store, run by the Captain). She considered them symbols of "women as objects to be dominated" and asked Capt. S. (who alternates with Captain Harvey) to take them down. He refused, saying that he was "proud" of them. A line of crewmembers was standing outside the slop chest at the time; the consensus is that Captain S. took a hard line to establish his authority. Had Laura approached him in private, she might have gotten her way.*

Here's how the case played out:

- Sea-Land reprimanded Captain S. but let him keep his job.
- Laura is now sailing Chief Mate with one of Sea-Land's rival companies, Matson Lines.
- Photos and calendars in *Endurance's* "public places" now feature wild animals of the jungle variety, travel posters, and maidens in long-necked kimonos.
- A notice has been thumbtacked to all the ship's bulletin boards, warning:
  IT HAS COME TO OUR ATTENTION THAT
  THERE MAY BE UNREPORTED CASES OF SEXUAL
  HARASSMENT WITHIN OUR ORGANIZATION.
  SEXUAL HARASSMENT IS NOT ONLY A
  VIOLATION OF SEA-LAND SERVICE'S COMPANY
  POLICY BUT A BREACH OF U.S. LAW. ANYONE
  VIOLATING THE POLICY MUST CEASE SUCH
  CONDUCT IMMEDIATELY OR BE SUBJECT TO

DISCIPLINE, UP TO AND INCLUDING DISCHARGE.

This harassment story leads me to Jess, the Second Engineer. I've been more curious about her than anyone else on the ship. Because of her age (thirty-seven; I peeked at her data sheet) and officer's status, I assume she's been around and has some tales to tell. At lunchtime, I ask her if we can chat after she gets off work.

The engineers live on the 04 deck, one below the deck officers. That puts them a level closer to the engine — which they take turns baby-sitting at night. Alarms in their staterooms alert them if something's awry. Jess's door is open, and I see she's hunching over a notebook computer much like mine; I'm jealous that her screen displays color. Other than on the day she signed on, I haven't seen her out of her coveralls. She's changed into a plain gray sweatshirt and well-worn jeans; her hair is still wet from the shower. "God, it feels great to de-slime," she says as she shakes her hair to help it dry.

I want to ask Jess a thousand questions, but when she points to the red alarm on the wall and tells me it's her night to "take the duty," I stick to the subject at hand: "Can you tell me what your career has been like, surrounded by men? Do you ever get hassled?"

She looks at me in disbelief. "What do you think, Nancy? I've been the brunt of jokes and obscenities. I've been groped, stalked and once had a First (Engineer) use his passkey to get into my room. Good thing he was a little guy; I beat him up. I think it's more than just being a bunch of horny guys; they get hostile if I do a better job than they. They hate being shown up by a woman; it affects their machismo.

"Can't tell you how many times I've slept with a knife under my pillow. My friend Helen packs a gun. By the way, Helen was a real pioneer and a role model for me. She was a single mother tending bar at a seaman's joint.

She said to herself, 'I'm smarter than any of these assholes,' went back to school, got her Third Mate's license and became a legend. She always said she was going to write a book called Sea Bitches.

Jess has dozens of stories. One of her buddies signed on as a cadet and was informed by her Captain, "You *will* be sleeping with me." The Second Mate, who'd seen the Captain pull this before, went to bat for her: arranged to get all her luggage off the ship, and with the aid of other crewmembers held the Captain's door shut while she ran away. Her Academy assigned her to another ship, and the Captain was fired.

And then there are the traditional sexual references aboard ship. With women aboard now, the rules have changed, but enforcement is often lacking. The tops of twistlocks (fist-sized metal pieces that fit into the corner castings of the containers and lock them together vertically) are still called "peckerheads" and the big, absorbent pads used to sop up oil, "Kotex."

And even though wise captains inform their female sailors as they come aboard, "If anyone gives you a hard time, you come to me immediately," this is often followed by, "By the same token, please don't start anything."

"Starting something" is fraught with danger. Some women have complained that if they hang around with one of the men, others get jealous. Rumors race through the ship that she's a whore. On the other hand, shipboard abstinence is read as lesbianism. Women also complain that they can't tack up "stud shots" in their rooms as the men hang up naked women in theirs, because word gets out that the female offenders are looking for action.

Likewise, women sailors must be more careful than males about casual remarks. No jokes about male organs or lecherous fellow workers. The gossip mill takes everything a woman says seriously, and stories about her can float from ship to ship. She may find her "reputation" precedes her as she climbs aboard a new vessel.

"People find me hard around the edges," Jess finishes, "so they probably won't believe that twenty years ago when I started engineering school, I was as timid as the cadet. But my ex-husband turned into a Mr. Hyde when he started drinking and three-quarters of the men I work with are on your case, so I had to form a protective shell. And since the life at sea will drive you crazy, it's better to ship out already deranged."

The containership M/V *Sea-Land Endurance.*

The author on *Endurance's* bridge-wing.

Chief Mate Bob Allen (Saeng Do Rock, off Pusan, South Korea, in the background).

The Chief Mate walking along a catwalk to check reefers (refrigerated containers) while the ship is at sea.

Winter storm, North Pacific.

The author tries on a survival suit.

The Chief Mate (left) on the bridge of *Endurance*, as the ship enters Dutch Harbor, Alaska.

A tug assisting *Endurance* on its approach to the terminal at Dutch Harbor.

The dock at Dutch Harbor.

On the approach to Unalaska, in the Aleutians.

Captain Harvey, off the Korean coast.

The diesel cylinder heads in *Endurance*'s engine room.

Pusan harbor, South Korea

A tug alongside *Endurance*, Kobe, Japan.

Shanghai: *Endurance* approaching the dock in the Huangpu River north of the city, with containers aft of the foremast and in foreground container stacking frames.

Keith, the radio operator, relaxes ashore in Kaohsiung, Taiwan.

The view astern between decks as the waves rise above the main deck, as the *Endurance* leaves the Aleutians.

A rainbow over the bow and the containers, as *Endurance* approaches the California coast.

The container terminal at Long Beach, California, *Endurance*'s home port, with the *Queen Mary* in the background.

Chapter 11

DECEMBER 4, LATER

Jess' comments about insanity at sea have forced me to re-examine the Chief Mate's life on Endurance. *The stress he suffers is incredible. Even though his shortest work day is around twelve hours (and that's every day; there's no such thing as a weekend or holiday off during the voyage), he's always behind. As the "super generalist," he tends the reefers though rain and snow, stands his two watches, navigates, trains the cadet and shifts the papers which seem to spread like viruses over his desk.*

I've started to develop a mild case of guilt and ask Bob if there's anything I can do to help. "How about taking these sign-on sheets and entering the data in my computer? I'll need an updated crew list for all the foreign ports," he says, with a small smile of relief.

It's a dream job because there are shipmates I haven't met yet — just glimpsed in the hallways and food line. I'll even be able to match faces with names because all the passport pictures have been photocopied.

Endurance carries a crew of twenty-one: Captain (abbreviated in the computer as "MAD," a symbol that means "Master, Dayworker"); Chief Mate; Second and Third Mates; Chief Engineer; First, Second and Third Engineers; Radio Operator;

Boatswain (Bosun); Electrician; QMED (Qualified Member Engine Department); Wiper; five Able Seamen; BR (Bedroom Steward); Steward/Baker and Chief Cook. The cadet is #22, and I have been designated as "Supernumerary," #23.

"Wiper" is a puzzling job description. The Chief Mate clarified, "The wiper, along with the BR, is the low man on the ship's totem pole, relegated to mopping up the engine room spills and chipping paint. Wipers often make claims against the company because number one, they're disgruntled with their work, and two, they're pissed off at the Chief Engineer ordering them around. They make a very low base wage but get a lot of overtime, working at night and on weekends."

The M/V *Endurance* is a mini melting pot. Her crew hails from all parts of the U.S. (including Hawaii), Yemen, the Philippines, Denmark and England — fair, olive, brown, and black. We have super-shapes like Ken and no shape at all like Louis. Our ages range from nineteen to eighty — the latter is Chris, the white-haired Bosun, who can still do handstands and other gymnastic feats. We are licensed and unlicensed; uneducated and over-educated (the Chief Mate has quipped that his Ph.D. comes in handy when he's cutting up old computer paper for scratch pads).

Twenty-one pairs of hands aren't very many to handle a behemoth ship. *Endurance* was originally designed for a crew of thirty-nine, but every stateroom on the 03 deck is now empty. Foreign competition has forced American shipping companies to pare down. Sea-Land pays a smaller crew more overtime rather than hiring "cheap" extra hands (whose unions extract substantial fringe-benefit costs from the shipping companies). The skeleton crew leaves no margin for error or illness. This includes hangovers; no one is available to cover for lapses of another. It seems that little has changed since Dana wrote, "Our merchant ships are always undermanned."

Monthly salaries range all over the place: from $10,834.23 a month for the "MAD" to $1,608.68 for an unlicensed AB and $1,341.22 for the BR. (On Dana's ship, an AB made $12 a month.) The Chief Mate is down for $4,874.23, but he takes home almost as much as the Captain. "Oh, I get a lot of overtime," he explains. "I used to 'donate' some of my extra hours but that was when Chief Mates didn't stand eight hours of watch a day. Now that I'm up-to-my-ass-in-alligators, I put in for every minute I'm on the job."

While the Chief Mate might make between $120,000 and $130,000 a year, about half of this is in overtime. However, his pension is based on straight time wages from a forty-hour work week. He has calculated that he'll be better off taking a lump sum buy-out when he retires and invests this large amount himself, rather than receiving a dole-out every year. The buy-out has the extra advantage of removing his hard-earned pension monies from union control.

The *Endurance*, as well as the other Sea-Land ships under the American flag, is manned by members of four unions:

(1) International Organization of Masters, Mates and Pilots (commonly known as "MM&P")
(2) Marine Engineer's Beneficial Association ("MEBA," pronounced "mee-ba")

(3) Seafarers International Union ("SIU"), for the unlicensed
    seamen
(4) Radio Operator's Union ("ROU")

Of the twenty-three bodies aboard, I suspect there are only three of us — the Captain, Ken and me — who really want to be out here. And I'm not too sure about Ken. Bob maintains, "It's no fun on these ships any more. We'd all be working ashore if we could make this kind of money." If I start having some fun, I'd better keep quiet about it.

Chapter 12

HALFWAY TO YOKOHAMA!

DECEMBER 5

Endurance is barreling along at her top speed of 21 knots or around 24 mph. I feel like an animal too long in the cave, confined by the weather. Time to break out. I grab one of the gray insulated jackets from the closet and make my way down the outside stairway to the main deck. The sea didn't look too rough from my porthole, but obviously that was an optical illusion. Once I'm on the main deck six stories down, the waves rolling in from the stern rise above me like jagged tors.

Still, I decide to Outward Bound it to the stern. I inch my way along the bouncing deck, praying there's enough tread on the old Nikes. A waist-high railing runs along the main deck, but it feels freaky to be that close to the water. So I hug the seven foot tall inboard pedestal the containers rest on. Unhappily, the ten to twenty ton boxes, taking up every available inch of space, overhang the passageway, about a foot above my skull. They ping, rattle, squeak and scrape; I don't dare look up. For extra excitement, the deck thunders under my feet the closer I get to the engine area. The noise alone kicks my heart into double-time. I should have told someone I was going for a walk in Reefer Park. I could fall and crack my cranium, get squashed by a container or fly overboard. Then I'd be dead of hypothermia in about five minutes, as I know too well from the Coast Guard film.

Still, some crazy quirk drives me to finish my walk, perhaps to prove to Bob, Jess, or Mr. Dana that I'm as brave as they are. Shaking from cold and fear, I make it through the tunnel of containers to the open afterdeck. But now I can see how high the waves really are — over thirty feet, I'd guess. If one breaks over the stern, it will sweep me into the sea. Enough of this so-called bravery.

I do a fast shuffle back to the stairway and climb panting up to my old perch on the 06 deck. Now I can look down at the sea, from a far less threatening vantage point than below. As Endurance struts her stuff, her bow waves shoot up like geysers. Over the milky turquoise wake, nets of foam swirl like a sea sprite's finger painting. From my now safe height, the seascape surrounds me with beauty, without a hint of danger. So much of life depends on perspective.

Well, no more outdoor excursions for me at these latitudes, even though I need to curb my restlessness and stop obsessing about getting off. I really shouldn't feel sorry for myself when I read about Dana's circumstances:

Miserable indeed . . . the forecastle shut up tight to keep out the water and cold air; the watch either on deck or asleep in their berths; no one to speak to; the pale light of a single lamp, swinging to and fro from the beam, so dim that one can scarcely see, much less read, by it; the water dripping from the beams and carlings and running down the sides, and the forecastle so wet and dark and cheerless, and so lumbered up with chests and wet clothes, that sitting up is worse than lying in the berth.

Perhaps my new project will curb the cabin fever. I've set up my notebook computer in a corner of the Chief Mate's office. While Bob is out fighting the reefers, I begin wrestling with "Windows." My son, the *software engineer, has insisted his mom learn to drive on the Information Highway. He selected a Toshiba ("very user-friendly") and installed Word for Windows ("just go through the tutorial"). However, the Toolbar I've been learning to use just vanished, probably forever like Jimmy Hoffa. So, I'll ponder my work space instead.*

The Chief Mate's office is a 12 × 14 room where the steel desk, file cabinets, computer shelf, and bookcases are all built-in. Even the orange Naugahyde couch is set in a steel frame. Cartons of unstowed supplies, videotapes, air tanks, life preservers, old logbooks, and survival suits overflow from the couch onto the floor. Scuff marks swirl over the vinyl tiles, and brown detritus has been waxed into the corners.

Two straightback chairs sit below a four-foot wide diagram of *Endurance's* holds and hatches, a map of the world's major shipping lanes and a twelve-inch level with an air bubble in magenta fluid marking the number of degrees the ship is listing. The Chief Mate's desk is covered with reefer and cargo manifests, manila envelopes, yellow reminder slips, crew overtime sheets, a short-wave radio. Buried underneath are photos of his boat, his cat, and his new wife.

My daily routine, which I fit around Bob's schedule, is as predictable as his. After the 1015–1030 coffee break, I tuck the C/M in for his Sleep Cycle (that's what the sign on his closed door pleads). The genius who redecorated the ship a few years back took away the light-tight curtains. Bob's brain needs the dark, even a fake one. So after he curls up, I adjust the covers over his eyes. I'm tempted to stay and stir up a little something, but even Kathleen Turner couldn't get him going when he's this sleep-deprived. The most he's able to muster is a whispered "Thanks, honey," before some hypnagogic mumbling, impossible to decode. He'll be out until I shake him awake at exactly 1245, and not a minute later.

Back to the computer. I watch the clock like a laborer and at exactly 1145, I run down for lunch. I've learned that Ed the Chief eats early (probably to avoid me) and is usually gone by now; Jess and Keith, the Radio Operator, arrive at the mess about the same time I do. After shooting the breeze with them, I make up something for Bob. On calm days he gets a bowl of soup with salad and fruit; when the ship is pitching (like today), it's a simple sandwich. That's because I have to maneuver a slick plastic tray through two steel doors at the 01 and 05 levels. They're three inches thick with massive hinges, and snap shut like clamshells when Endurance lurches. It was Amin, my protective little BR, who warned me, "You be careful with doors, Miz Allen. AB lost two fingers last trip."

Though I suspect Bob would rather dig into peanut butter and ice cream (his after-nap snack when he's alone on the ship), he never complains about the healthy food I bring him. During these fifteen minutes of rare luxury, he eats propped up in bed while I spin stories like Scheherezade. I tell him about Jess: "She's started to open up to me about her personal life. Her passion is an aerobatic Piper airplane, a red Super Cub. So that explains the Earhart hair. When I told her she might inspire me to start ground school, she said mysteriously, 'Then I won't tell you what happened to my first plane.' "

Most of my gossip is courtesy of Keith the Radio Operator; all the incoming messages (except faxes, which come into the Captain's office) pass by his eyes and ears. He dispenses tidbits as if they were dessert candies: there's another storm brewing up; a ship in trouble has activated its EPIRB (a device that sends out a distress signal) so the folks on the bridge are looking for flares; our ETA for Yokohama, Japan, has been extended by two hours because of the storm. Keith's relay of the missives spreads through the ship like tide gushing though a narrow channel.

By 1300 sharp, Bob is back at his desk. The cadet is already waiting, sitting straight and alert, for the afternoon's instructions. The two of them move over to my side of the room where an old AT computer wheezes out its final days. The AT receives a half hour of cursing while Bob searches for the right floppy disk and then discovers, "Someone from the last voyage fucked with my setup." Ken, wisely, keeps his mouth shut but scarlet cheeks tell me he'd rather be somewhere else. Finally, they get the program running, and Bob begins maneuvering Ken though a maze of minutiae.

It's part of a Merchant Marine cadet's training to work on requisition lists, overtime sheets, the program that calculates the ship's stability and draft, official forms for all the different ports and a schedule of maintenance and repairs to be made in Japan, Taiwan and Long Beach. I have the feeling, seeing Ken's bewildered expression, that they don't cover all of this at the Academy.

The second coffee break comes at 1500 (3 P.M.). These break periods for the crew are not to be fooled with; they're written into the union contracts. In the old days, officers took coffee breaks as religiously as the unlicensed, but now Chief Mates are too busy working three jobs: monitoring reefers, standing watch and tending to the ship's business. On those rare afternoons when Bob can steal away for fifteen minutes, I go work out and leave the C/M and the Captain to tell sea stories in the officer's lounge.

Yes, the Merchant Marine does believe in a sound body. It gives the officers a workout room, even if it is about the size of a closet. Crammed into it are an Exercycle, a rusty rowing machine, a gleaming NordicTrack, barbells and a bench, one of those pull-down weight machines and a water cooler. Bob warned me that the Captain paid for the NordicTrack with his own money so "you better not break it." Break it? I'm not even going to touch it. I hope the engine gets more oil than the rowing machine; it strains my arm sockets after sixty seconds. That leaves the bike, which works OK but is so boring. I can see why there used to be pinups for distraction. (I lust

after what's taken their place: a poster of the Hong Kong skyline at night.)
So I read from some more Merchant Marine material I picked up in the
lounge, while pedaling furiously in place:

> *The United States Merchant Marine emerged from the conflict of*
> *World War II, after having lost more than 6,000 mariners and 733*
> *cargo ships, carrying 60 percent of the world's tonnage across the seas.*
> *But coastal shipping was down, due to the greater flexibility of trucking*
> *and better highways. When containerization was introduced in the*
> *1950s, it spelled the beginning of the end of the conventional cargo ship,*
> *although the moribund fleet of break-bulk ships didn't disappear until the*
> *late 60s. Mechanized shipping eliminated inefficient loading and un-*
> *loading of freight, pilferage on the docks (in some ports, right and left*
> *shoes were shipped separately), or the ships' booms ruining the cargo.*
>
> *While the modern containerships may lack the romance of the old*
> *tramps and cargo liners, their beauty lies in their sheer bulk, power and*
> *efficiency. One of today's large containerships could carry the entire*
> *bulk of Queen Elizabeth I's merchant fleet.*

I kiss Bob good-bye as he leaves for his 1600 watch. Chief Mates on
containerships never stood watches until the mid-1980s, when the shipping
companies decided to save money by getting rid of an extra Third Mate
and shelling out more work and overtime to the remaining three Mates. For
his dinner break, Bob gets relieved by Bill, the Third Mate, for a half-hour.
In this short interval, he runs down seven stories from the bridge to the
galley, stands in the chow line, eats, and sprints back. For me at five in the
afternoon, it's too much food, too early. And not a drop of wine to whet
the appetite. But in two days, like the rest of the crew, I'll be drinking
ashore!

Chapter 13

DECEMBER 5, LATER

After I bus our dishes from the 5 P.M. feeding, I join Bob on the bridge. This quiet interlude is like an out-take from an otherwise frantic day. The Captain is still at the dinner table, munching methodically through several plates of veggies. Vince, the AB who's on the 4 to 8 watch with Bob, is content to stand outside the door to the bridge-wing and drag on one Marlboro after another, as the Captain won't allow smoke near his lungs or the bridge instruments. Since the Chief Mate doesn't have to plot a fix and write in the logbook for another twenty minutes, we have a few moments to sip coffee, look for a sunset in the washed-out pink on the horizon, the only vestige of ZELDA left, and share a cozy silence.

When the Captain comes up around 1850 (6:50) for his last regular check of the day, and to write the night's orders in the logbook, I know enough to get out of the way. An irresistible popcorn smell draws me to the officers' lounge; I find Ken the cadet watching a western on the VCR. I must look like a cat after catnip because he apologizes, "I'm sorry, Ma'am; I'd offer you some but I'm down to the bottom of the dish."

While I pop more golden kernels, I pick up a couple of Sea-Land newsletters lying on the table. Along with employee profiles, news of a cargo contract with Russia, and hype about an in-house "Quality

Program," there's material about the company that helps fill in some of my blanks:

In 1986, Sea-Land and its fleet of custom containerships merged with the railroad conglomerate CSX — and so began a new phase with a high-tech name: INTERMODALISM. It's an integrated truck/rail/ship system, whereby a shipper can get his product from Point A to Point B with just one bill of lading. The newsletter described how it works:

> Ashley Furniture of Arcadia, Wisconsin, is the leading importer of unassembled furniture from the Far East. Sea-Land ships the containers to Tacoma, Washington; then they travel over two railroad lines (Burlington Northern and Wisconsin Central) to Arcadia. There, Ashley unloads the unassembled material and reloads the containers with finished furniture, which CSX moves over its railroad network to Ashley's distribution centers in the Northeast, Southeast and West Coast. In all, Ashley empties and refills 50 containers a week.

This all sounds groovy, good company PR, but there are hard problems that the handout ignores. Cheap, non-union labor abroad versus high operating costs at home have resulted in 95 percent of the oceangoing cargo entering or leaving the United States moving on foreign-flagged ships. U.S. shipowners are abandoning the American flag to register their vessels under "flags of convenience" in Vanuatu (formerly the New Hebrides), Belize and the Marshall Islands. The world's largest fleet now flies the Panamanian flag.

How is it that America's Merchant Marine has tumbled from the summit of sea power so soon after its glory days? U.S. government taxes and stringent regulations play a part, but I suspect the main cause of the slow death of American shipping is the maritime unions. They have demanded wages beyond what the shipping companies can afford, to remain competitive in the global marketplace.

I have a bit of baggage to bring to the table on this subject. My father, son of a German butcher, worked his way through law school and was engaged to my mother for six years until they could afford to marry. He believed in honest, hard work and hated handouts, corruption and unions. And now, I'm married to a union man and worse, one who has a waterfront house, a sailboat, first-rate medical insurance and pension plan.

Bob credits his union, "Masters, Mates and Pilots," for his good salary and benefits. Maritime unions have also provided protection for their seamen from exploitive masters and shipping companies, and eliminated the inhumane conditions that still exist aboard some foreign ships. And yet, here's the paradox: the decent wages the unions have negotiated for their members have caused U.S. flag ships to use smaller crews working longer hours to save money, or turn to foreign flagging.

The American farmer has been a highly vocal critic of seamen's wages. Farmers complain that agricultural cargo must be carried by U.S. ships, which costs them more than flag-of-convenience vessels. Meanwhile, agriculture remains one of the country's most subsidized industries. Another paradox.

DECEMBER 6

Can it be true? We're only a day away from foreign terra firma! Even if I hadn't heard it from Keith the Radio Operator, I'd have figured out from the activity on the ship that something was up. The Laser Jet printer is spitting out forms. The laundry room's awash with damp clothes, waiting for the one dryer. Several beards have disappeared from crew faces. Vince's flowing hair looks conditioned; he's bragging his rich Japanese girlfriend will be waiting on the dock in Yokohama.

I've heard about the "slop chest," and curiosity gets the better of me. I join the long line of crewmen slouching against the wall outside the Captain's office. Following an old shipboard custom, Captain Harvey opens up the small storeroom once a week. Much like a druggist, he stands behind a counter and sells cigarettes, cases of Coke, Calistoga Water, and O'Doul's non-alcoholic beer; toiletries; Endurance T-shirts, caps, and mugs; candy bars and peanuts. I get up the courage to ask him why no condoms. He looks embarrassed: "Well, um . . . we don't get into that."

"Well, why not? What about AIDS?" I'm about to ask, but recall Dana's words just in time, "The captain . . . is accountable to no-one and must be obeyed in everything." And that is still true.

At the same time, Captain Harvey gives out cash advances against salary, or "draws." I overhear George the electrician tell Nagi the wiper, "I'm takin' out $500 — that'll buy me a couple of Nipponese beers." When we packed up, Bob warned me to bring enough shampoo, deodorant, toothpaste and Tampax to last through Japan. "It's outrageously expensive over there; even a cup of coffee costs three dollars," he said. "I hope you're not expecting too much."

What does he mean? How much will it cost to look around and take pictures? I guess Bob doesn't know that most of my clothes come from thrift shops, though he should remember my old Camry is pushing 120,000 miles. Besides, how could I possibly be disappointed? I'm halfway around the world. I've survived twelve days at sea with a ship full of strangers. I should be ready to take on the Japanese!

PART III

"Fast-Forwarding the Far East"

We must come down from our heights, and leave our straight paths for the byways and low places of life, if we would learn truths by strong contrasts; and in hovels, in forecastles, and among our own outcasts in foreign lands, see what has been wrought among our fellow-creatures by accident, hardship, or vice.

Richard Henry Dana

Chapter 14

PORT OF YOKOHAMA, HONSHU ISLAND, JAPAN

DECEMBER 7

It's unsettling to sense Endurance *slowing down; I've grown used to the rhythm of her heart, the engine, at 120 beats a minute. And it's eerie to see mounds of reddish land poking up from the seascape; the sea — even in its worst moods — has become oddly comfortable. Like a space traveler re-entering Planet Earth, I'm apprehensive as I peer out the big windows on the bridge, watching the headlands dotted with lighthouses and hotels give way to storage tanks and smokestacks. They're belching billows of black smoke.*

The harbor of Yokohama, protected by a giant breakwater from the bay that continues north to Tokyo, is lined with other breakwaters and piers, containerships and cranes, lighters and tugs. This is the legacy, as well as the historic path, of Commodore Perry and his black-hulled steam frigates. A century and a half ago, Perry with his "black fleet" opened Japan to outside trade (a Shogunate had kept it under strict isolation for two hundred years). Back then, Yokohama was a hamlet of only one hundred peasant families. It expanded with the silk trade, then suffered two major declines: first, after an earthquake in 1923 that killed fifty thousand people, and then during the World War II bombing raids. The city rebuilt to become the world's third-largest seaport. The guidebook is unexpectedly blunt about it: "Today, Yokohama is a manufacturing powerhouse filled with more choking smog than romantic mist."

Ferries, tiny fishing boats with steadying sails and U.S. Navy ships share our waters as we approach the port. Overhead, airplanes and helicopters buzz about. The terminal itself is all concrete, containers and cranes; the noise is earsplitting and the air smells like the steel mill smoke I choked on back in Pittsburgh.

The half-dozen dock men handling Endurance's *lines are done up in identical khaki uniforms, with white trouser guards, boots, helmets and gloves. They look like the militia instead of scruffy extras from* On the Waterfront. *The line handlers' polished look is echoed by jaunty green and white tugs, freshly painted and spotless. Even Sea-Land's local operations manager, Mr. Matsui, is dressed to impress. He comes aboard to pick up port papers wearing a tweed jacket, striped shirt and tie, pleated pants and polished loafers. Only his insistent bowing reminds me I'm not at home.*

A little after 8 P.M., Bob tells me "This is one of the rare times when the timing is perfect. I'm off watch now, everything is in order, the shore passes are ready, and Captain Harvey has offered you his bike. We'll go to the Seamen's Club and pick up some yen; then I'll take you to Chinatown for dinner."

Worried about the Captain's bike getting stolen, I ask Bob about a chain when we disembark at the Club. He informs me, "You never see a bicycle locked up here; Japanese honor, you know." I'm amazed: it's a city of three million people!

It seems like half of those millions are in the Seamen's Club; it's full of Japanese men in black suits. Bob explains, "They like to come here, drink American beer, eat fried chicken, listen to country music . . ." And chain-smoke.

"Bob, can we just exchange money, mail these letters, and split?" I plead, pointing to my red eyes. When the envelopes weigh in to the tune of $26, I gulp. I never dreamed postage would be as expensive as the other stuff I was warned about. Bob's frown turns to resignation: "I forgot to tell you. In Okinawa we can use U.S. postage. But go ahead and mail the letters. I know how much you miss your buddies."

In Chinatown, where Bob says he won't have to trade a month's salary for dinner, we find a point-to-order menu in a window. We're the only Caucasians in the big communal dining room, but no one looks up from his bowl. Such concentration! Such slurping! We too suck up noodles con brio, hunched-over like our three aged tablemates.

Out on the street, I feel a cooler wind and smell cleaner air. I jump on the bike with new vigor and resolve, the breeze at my back like a helping hand. Bob, who missed all but an hour of his morning nap, seems energized too. Pedaling back, I smile at my fantasy: that we're having a real honeymoon and will park the bikes by a pink bungalow on a Caribbean beach.

STILL DOCKED AT YOKOHAMA

DECEMBER 8

I didn't hear Bob's 3 A.M. wake-up call, so when the phone rings and I see daylight, it's a shock. "Chief Mate here. Hurry up to the bridge!" Throwing a jacket over my sweat suit and not bothering with shoes, I run up the stairs.

Bob doesn't say a word but points to starboard. "What? It's a beautiful day . . . it's great to see the sun . . . but why the big rush?" "Look UP," Bob directs and I follow his finger halfway up the sky, about where I usually find Orion after dark. A monster cone with a pure white top sits there, as if a stagehand came during the night and painted it onto the blue backdrop.

"I didn't want to tell you about Mount Fuji," Bob confesses, "because I've seen it just once in all my trips. The only time it appears is after a cold front blows the smog out, then it's gone as soon as the factories fire up. Sorry to wake you up, but this is probably going to be it."

When I come back a few minutes later with my camera, half of Fujiyama has already been swallowed up by smog. If there are gods on this most-sacred mountain, they've decided to withdraw behind the smoke-screen we mortals have manufactured.

Mr. Matsui, the operations manager, sits next to Bob at breakfast. He's piled up two plates with scrambled eggs, bacon and sausage, pancakes, toast and a cheese Danish. Since he's thin, I suppose he doesn't dabble in American cuisine regularly. I ask Mr. Matsui, whose English is more than passable, "Do you think I can get to the city by myself? Last night I didn't see any signs in English, and I don't know the yen system yet."

"No sweat," he replies. "You get #26 bus in front of Seamen's Club and go — let see — seven stops to Sakuragicho Station. Across street is beautiful new development on old Mitsubishi land. Here (he plops a pocketful of coins on the table) — I teach you yen."

I get a nervous hug from Bob, along with a firm admonition, "We're scheduled to sail at 1500 and everyone must be aboard by 1400. Have Mr. Matsui write down the ship's location in Japanese, in case you get stranded." Directions and yen in hand, I set off stoutly for the unknown.

The bus is prompt, and the 200 yen I hand the driver is accepted without comment. Sakuragicho Station appears on schedule; it even has a Japanese/English sign. Across from the Station an Asian Emerald City offers up modernistic glass skyscrapers, a giant Ferris wheel and a spider web of construction cranes. Mr. Matsui told me to go to the tallest building — the Landmark Tower — first, and there at the Information Desk, I find I've stepped into the future.

The name of this mini-city, says the bilingual brochure, is Minato Mirai 21 ("Future Port Twenty-First Century"). It will occupy 460 acres of prime waterfront property. The Tower, designed by the American architect Hugh Stubbins, rises seventy stories, the highest building in Japan. Designed to withstand earthquakes and typhoon winds, its interior atrium ends somewhere in the clouds.

The brochure describing Minato Mirai highlights an observation deck atop of the Landmark Tower, two swank hotels, fine arts and maritime museums. I decide to see it all, the caricature of a crazed tourist.

The quartet of young ladies who orchestrate the elevator ride to the observatory are dressed identically, clones of a '60s Jackie Kennedy in pink suits and pillbox hats, black pumps and white gloves. Glossy black pageboys, high-pitched voices, ceaseless smiles and little bows complete the modern geisha effect. They soothe the faint-of-heart while the elevator rockets up sixty-nine floors in forty seconds.

The art museum is crammed with exquisite ancient-to-modern works but is nearly devoid of people. They've migrated to the Inter-Continental coffee shop, to consume artful pastries. I join them, ordering a strawberry tart with rice cracker crust and tea in a fragile flowered cup. The sugar and caffeine fix propels me through the Maritime Museum, where dioramas, films and interactive displays unfold the complex history of the Port. A video camera, mounted somewhere high up, can be controlled by the visitor to sweep around 360°. Incredibly, I'm able to zoom over to Endurance and spot small figures walking around the deck. When I get back, I will tell the C/M that at 1230, I observed him reading Playboy when he should have been watching the cargo.

Short on time and yen (admission fees and the little snack have eaten up almost $50), I hurry back to the bus stop. I pray the #26 bus driver will get the message when I hand him Mr. Matsui's paper. He turns and waves his arm when the Seamen's Club comes in view. I clamber aboard Endurance with forty minutes to spare, sighing with relief that her S/L smokestack still dominates the terminal — and that Bob awaits at the top of the gangway.

At the main deck office, I notice a striking woman on the young side of forty, sitting straight in a chair and dressed all in black: fur jacket, turtleneck, short shirt and knee-high boots. "Are you Michiko?" I ask, because she has to be Vince's girlfriend. She nods, smiling. "And you, Mrs. Chief Mate. Sorry, English not good. I say good-bye to Vincent." She holds out a Seaman's Card, showing a much younger Vince, with shorter hair and no earring. "Very handsome," we agree.

Since I know exactly one word of Japanese ("arigato" — thank you), I'm glad when Vince returns and I can exit with a bow — a gesture which, after my first day in Japan, has become an automatic reflex.

Vince has told the Chief Mate about Michiko in bits and pieces during the long night watches. Though the guys would never admit it, they — like those early sailors in the forecastle — form friendships through the spinning of yarns.

Michiko is still in an arranged marriage to a successful Tokyo architect; but she's unhappy, mostly because they haven't had sex for six years. Her maid liked to hang out at the Seamen's Club and brought her employer there, where Vince entered the picture. Now every time his ship lands in Japan, Michiko whisks him off in her Mercedes coupe. (He switches his shipboard watches with another AB who prefers his liberty in Hong Kong.)

The arrangement suits them perfectly. Vince got burned by marriage once and is not eager to try again; Michiko can play her wifely role and get enough allowance to buy her lover lavish gifts, like the Italian gold watch he flashes. He's also acquiring her jewelry: that rock in his earlobe used to weigh down Michiko's finger.

Almost to the minute, twenty-four hours after docking in Yokohama, the green and white tugs reappear to pull Endurance *away. The ship and I are hurrying off to Kobe — where more Japanese wait for more Alaskan fish.*

Chapter 15

ROKKO ISLAND, KOBE

DECEMBER 9

For the next couple of weeks, we'll be in "the loop" as the crew calls it: coastal shipping between ports in the Far East. Endurance will exchange cargo six times between Japan and Hong Kong. Some of her discharged containers are picked up by smaller feeder ships, which transport it locally.

Most of the crew — and Supernumerary — relish this part of the voyage with its shoreside "liberty." But not the Chief Mate. His life will be complicated by dockings that devour more of his meager sleep, supervising the new cargo, and preparing the mass of paperwork each port requires. There is one plus: after Japan, the reefer load will be reduced by half.

A squad of seven Japanese mechanics came aboard in Yokohama; during the eighteen-hour period between Yoko and Kobe, they've been working around the clock to rebuild a generator. They're small and wiry as adolescents, and should stay that way, since they brought along their own healthy food. Everyone marched up the gangway in identical clean blue coveralls and white work gloves. Then they disappeared into the engine room. Jim, the First Engineer, reports that they're working away like one body with fourteen hands.

The Kobe pilot has made it up the Jacob's ladder without soiling his pinstripe suit and white gloves. (Captain Harvey's fashion statement: well-worn khakis and jogging socks with red stripes.) The pilot shouts kung fu-style to the helmsman: TWO! SIX! ZERO! I glance at the Captain, puzzled. He translates, "Steer a course of two hundred and sixty degrees." Though the Captain retains ultimate authority for his ship, he stands discreetly behind the pilot while Endurance dodges other ships in the channel. Bob whispers, "Japanese harbor pilots take home several hundred thousand dollars a year. When one of my female cadets heard this, she asked the pilot if he was single."

Unlike Yokohama, Kobe presents a beautiful profile toward the sea. The city's core follows a curving shoreline, low mountains behind it trace an arched outline against the sky. We glide past the downtown area to Rokko Island jutting offshore. Bob tells me that Rokko and an adjacent island called Port are the two largest man-made islands in the world. Each one is built on a thousand acres of fill brought down from the mountains. He adds, "I know you'll love Rokko. It's so easy to get around — we don't even need bikes — and everything is done with such flair."

It's a perfect day for walking, crisp and sunny. We pass through a commercial section next to the container terminal; on a sidewalk in front of a Kirin brewery sit cases of beer, unchained and unattended. Too bad about that Japanese honor system. We press on, climbing a flight of stairs to an elevated park on top of a grassy berm. "This sure makes sense to me," Bob remarks. "The greenbelt separates the commercial and residential areas, while forming a noise barrier."

"I always hang out here," Bob says, stopping at an empty fenced-in yard, part sand, part concrete. Swings, slides and jungle gyms — painted in primary colors — wait at one end. "You have to be patient, but sooner or later they'll come," he continues. We're lucky: in a few minutes, a line of small children marches silently into the courtyard. The boys wear navy *blue suits and caps; the girls look like miniature ladies in white blouses, plaid skirts, black tights, and straw hats.*

Bob laughs, "I'm enchanted by these kids . . . they're so adorable and well-behaved. Sometimes one of the boys leads them around like the Pied Piper, banging on a drum. But I've gotten some dirty looks from the teachers; they probably think I'm a pedophile."

If I were to lay out Utopia, it might look something like downtown Rokko Island. There are low-rises, high-rises and skyscrapers, all different yet subtly harmonious. Styles stolen from Bauhaus, Post-Modern and Art Deco design. A piece of sculpture decorating every street corner. The Chief Mate's favorite: a marble bench with a bas relief schoolgirl teasing her cat with a ball of string. Winding walkways, stepped landscaping, flags and fountains add splash, as do the Rokko Islanders. Leaving the dark suits at home, they stroll around in brightly patterned clothes.

Even the public restrooms have style, making you realize why some Japanese regard Americans as barbarians. They're all immaculate, as if a maid had just cleaned up. You often find a ruffled brocade cover on the toilet paper holder. There's usually one sit-down john and one Asian bowl-in-the-floor model. But I've noticed in the newer buildings and hotels it's three to one in favor of the former. You never have to worry — you can find a bathroom anywhere, clearly marked with man-in-pants and woman-in-skirt symbols.

Bob and I are on a mission. At breakfast, Captain Harvey gave us some yogurt he'd picked up in Yokohama. The first taste was like a first kiss:

smooth and sweet, yet a little tart, so immediately addictive it should have been outlawed. I had to have more.

Besides the special yogurt, Rokko Island's supermarket features ingredients like Indian curries, New York cheesecake, French escargots, and Italian pastas. The smell of hot peanut oil signals a tempura bar. Next to it is a seafood section with row after row of purple octopus. Lining another wall, packages of meat glow a bright chemical red. Since everything is written in Japanese, it's difficult to figure out which, if any, is the famous "Kobe beef."

Food prices are shocking. Apples cost three dollars each and honeydews sixteen. Happily, the yogurt is a bargain at less than two dollars for a two-cup container.

Bob agrees we should buy as many yogurts as I can cram in my backpack. At the same time, he looks at his watch for the fourth time. "I'm sorry, baby, I have to get ready for my watch. But why don't you do some more exploring?"

After Bob takes off with the heavy backpack, and I figure I can find my way back to Endurance by foot, I feel truly unencumbered. I spot the big "S" of a Sheraton Hotel and wander over. On the mezzanine, a hefty blond fellow presides over a piano bar. I jump at hearing "Nancy!" and turn to find Keith the Radio Operator lounging on a plum velour couch. The glass table in front holds a half-dozen empty Heineken bottles and two full ashtrays. "Sit down, girl; I'll get you a drink. Have to trek up to the bar . . . they won't bring it over."

As Keith waddles off in his dirty hunting jacket, laced-up boots, and patched jeans, I spot two Japanese women watching him, frowning. They're dressed in Chanel-style suits, silk blouses and classic black pumps. I'm chuckling when Keith returns with a green bottle in each hand; "Keith, I just figured out that gaijin doesn't mean foreign devil at all; it's really "guy-in-jeans." What is not so funny: they are being served and we are not.

I tell my tablemates about it at dinner. Captain Harvey nods empathically. "We used to call at the port of Hakata. On our maiden voyage there, the mayor threw a reception for the officers and gave me the keys to the city. Miss Hakata, who could have been Olive Oyl's twin, presented me with one of their famous dolls. And that night I was thrown out of a bar: "Japanese only!" they informed me.

"You know, Captain," Bob interjects, "Vince checked that story out with Michiko. She says yes, that does happen but not because of racism. Japanese businessmen would be mortified if a gaijin saw them staggering around drunk."

DECEMBER 10

Today will be a test of courage, and even more: navigation skills. My goal is the shopping street (called the "Motomachi") in downtown Kobe — by train. I'm nervous about it, because Rusty warned me it's easy to catch the wrong train; he once had to pay sixty dollars for a cab back from Osaka. This would not please the Chief Mate.

Part One entails taking an elevated tram from Rokko Island over to the mainland, and there transferring to the main-line railroad. Yesterday in the Sheraton, I spotted a symbol of a train engine (a little "face" with lights for eyes) with an arrow above it. So I follow it up an escalator and onto a platform cantilevered out from the hotel. A machine displays multiple numbers but no English. I feed in the maximum number of yen, grab the ticket that pops out and hope for the best.

Whew . . . the tram dead-ends at the train station. But now what? A wall diagram of rail routes is beautifully color-coded — but all in Japanese. I ask the guard standing stiffly beside it, "English?" He shakes his head without a smile. I'm back to puzzling over the map when a plump lady with a British accent taps me on the arm and asks, "Can I help you, dear?" I must look totally helpless because she leads me to an upper level and shows me the track to wait by. She gives me a reassuring pat, along with the number of stops to count and the blocks to walk.

The Motomachi would not be easy to find on your own. A dog-leg from the train stop and down an alleyway, a long corridor opens up. It isn't a street at all, but a mile-long walkway, topped by a glass arch and lined on both sides with boutiques and stalls. Like our American malls, it's filled with a mixture of the tacky (souvenirs) and the elegant (Louis Vuitton bags and bolts of shimmering silk).

I get out my calculator, planning to buy Bob a new belt. I find a very nice one — for 1200 yen ($120). I pass. Nor do I really need that $1,300 suede jacket or the $2,400 suit. I'm surprised to find a table-full of books in English in a little bookstore. I pick up a collection of humorous photos from Life and am chuckling away when a woman my age comes over and asks, "Can I see please what is funny?" It isn't her English that startles me as much as her kimono — the first one I've seen close-up. I stare at the lush mixture of colors and patterns, wondering why the Japanese would trade these exquisite outfits for the drab western suits which seem to be the downtown uniform.

I leave the Motomachi empty-handed, and steer myself back to Rokko Island. I'm starving and parched, looking for a drink to wash down the peanut butter sandwich I'd packed. Two vending machines sit side by side on a corner: one containing "Pocari Sweat" and "Jolt Cola"; the other, cans of Kirin. Disinclined to sweat or jolt, I drop in 150 yen for the familiar beverage, guaranteed to mellow.

Safely back, I'm bursting to tell Bob about my excursion. But he begs, "Later, okay? I'm in the middle of figuring the ship's stability. This is *probably the most critical thing I do, which happens every time new containers come on."*

The shoreside Marine Department provides the Chief Mate with a print-out of the cargo plan. He plugs the cargo weights into his shipboard program, called CARGOMAX. He also enters the weights of liquids stored in various tanks: marine diesel fuel, HFO (heavy fuel oil), fresh water, and saltwater ballast.

Principally, what he's after is the sailing draft (how deep the ship sits in the water fore and aft) and a numerical value that measures the ship's stability. Specifically, this latter value is the distance between G (the center of gravity of ship and cargo) and M (the metacenter), measured in feet. The metacenter is an imaginary pivot point around which the ship rolls, similar to the way a pendulum works. If the G ever moved above the M, negative stability would result and *Endurance* could roll over and keep right on going. Practically, the ship always has positive stability, but ironically, the lower the stability, the better she rides.

Here at the dock, the ship has a bad list to port. The Chief Mate will instruct the engineers to pump out one of the saltwater tanks used for controlling list. The discharged water, about to mingle with that of Rokko Island's, could have come from anywhere. With ships in international waters regularly pumping out and filling their ballast tanks, the interchange of water-borne organisms has become an international concern.

We're scheduled to sail right after dinner, and Mr. Itoh, like his Yokohama cohort, is wolfing down one last American meal: a hunk of roast beef framed in fat, french fries, baked potato with sour cream, canned peas, and two pieces of Sara Lee cheesecake. He has also left a little gift — a calendar. I flip through the pages: very young women with very small breasts, eyes averted from the camera. But the pubic parts have been airbrushed out, making the models resemble half-aliens. Not so Miss December, boldly baring all on our stateroom wall. She "belongs" to the other Chief Mate, Bob assures me.

Endurance casts off at sunset. The Kobe skyline is even lovelier at twilight: the city lights slope up slightly from the edge of the water, then disappear at the point where the land sharply steepens. Lights of lesser intensity, emanating from a thousand houses, twinkle at the mountain crests like stars that have fluttered to earth.

Sadly, this is the end of exploring Japan, for now. I plan to return to this country — the size of California, where the literacy rate is 99 percent — filled with so many paradoxes. From the word "Maru," which for thousands of years has been attached to ships' names to mean "perfect" or "complete," to the current craze of importing Australian girls to work as modern geishas, the culture fascinates. Even more, the lifestyle attracts me. The efficiency, artistry and less-is-more attitude is 180° from my life at home, which consists of projects-in-pieces, bushels of junk mail, spare boat parts overflowing into the house. Oh to live in a pristine space, with sculpture for streetlights. And leave my car unlocked.

Chapter 16

THE SEA OF JAPAN, APPROACHING KOREA

DECEMBER 11

Coming up for coffee after dinner, I pull apart the thick curtains that separate the forward bridge from the chart area, and I'm flabbergasted. The sea, which has been black and barren during the nights since Kobe, is filled with blazing lights! And we're still one hundred miles off the coast of Korea. "What is this, Close Encounters?"

"A fleet of squid fishermen," Bob explains. "They rig huge floodlights on their boats, which draw the little devils up to the surface. I've never seen how they actually catch the squid . . . I'm always too busy trying to zigzag around them."

The floodlights are so bright they hurt my eyes; it's like looking at a dozen suns. But I'm curious enough about them to stare as we skirt by a modern steel vessel of eighty feet. The lights are mounted on a framework strung around the deck. I've heard that making money catching fish is really tough. I wonder how I'd feel if I saw a foreign flagged monster hull plowing through my fishing grounds.

I turn from the boats and walk back to the chart area. Since I first started to sail, I've found nautical charts romantic, exciting, but these Korean islands and harbors have sing-songy names like "Gageog Do," "Dadae Po," "Dong Gu," "Yongdang Dong," and "Daemong Bong." Exciting maybe, romantic, not! Over the VHF radio, the Korean voices sound like they're tuning up for Karaoke.

An E-mail sheet has been clipped to the Chief Mate's office door:

FROM: WG RYU
TO: SLENDRNC
good morning, capt.
welcome your new deployment for Pusan call
1. your berth is best available from/to 130900/132300
2. your eta pus is 120800 noted but berth is not avail till 130900 so, pls proceed to pus outer harbor roads limit and await our further notice.

I ask Bob for a translation. "The message is from Mr. Ryu, Sea-Land's cargo manager in Pusan. He's telling us that, as usual, dock space won't be available until tomorrow. That's because South Korea's cargo-handling needs — importing frozen food and exporting Samsung TVs and Gold Star computers — has outgrown its ports."

I didn't know that ships of Endurance's size anchored. I ask permission to tag along for the operation, since I haven't seen the bow — hidden as it is by a thousand containers. We walk forward along the main deck, boxes hanging over our heads like a steel canopy, before dead-ending at a high bulkhead. A narrow ladder slopes upward. We climb the ladder, run into another steel bulkhead, turn a sharp corner. And there, like a secret compartment, lies the bow.

The triangular area is the size of a condo. Mounted on the chipped red deck are enormous wheels, levers and bitts; ropes and chains lie coiled like sleeping pythons. The anchors themselves are carried outboard, with their shafts thrust up inside the hawsepipes on either side. Most amazing of all, two people — the Chief Mate and Chris, the octogenarian Bosun — are poised to anchor forty thousand tons of steel.

The Chief Mate and Captain speak back and forth on the walkie-talkies. "Both anchors ready, Captain." "Okay, Bob . . . starboard anchor . . . five shots in the water." (Shots are ninety-foot lengths of chain, connected by shackles.) Bob then shouts to Chris, "Let go, Bosun!" As Chris puts leverage on a steel wheel that disgorges chain from a locker below deck, he warns me, "Stand back!" No problem there; I jump like a flea when the chain flies out, coughing up a cloud of rust and dried mud. That's why half the Bosun's face is covered with goggles. As the links — each of them more than a foot long — pass over a drum, they beat out a thunderous rhythm like a heavy-metal band.

The whole operation, from arrival to securing the anchor, takes an hour; then, stillness. With the engine shut down, gone are the pulsating pistons and clanking containers. I could be back on my old sailboat, swinging quietly at anchor. And yet, waiting for sleep, I find the silence unsettling. It's as if the ship has stopped breathing. I want the engine's rhythm back — and most of all, my vibrating bed.

AT ANCHOR OFF PUSAN

DECEMBER 12

The breakfast bunch is discussing the weather: an unusual mild spell. The Captain tells me, "In the wintertime, we usually get weather that roars across

Russia, then slams into Korea. We call it the 'Siberian Express.' You should take advantage of today; I think Sparks has a deck chair stashed somewhere."

I set up the chair in the lee of the smokestack, roll up the sleeves of my windbreaker, rub on some sunscreen, and take in the scene. Bob had told me that I'd see Golden Rock off the port bow and there it is, a tall jagged clump that looks as menacing as it is. Pusan, a couple of miles away, reminds me of St. Thomas in the Virgin Islands: high mountains, brown in the dry season, rising sheer out of the sea. Columns of high-rises zigzag up the slopes; the city below nestles around a natural harbor. From its mouth, ships loaded with cargo scurry back and forth, like trucks on I-95.

I feel somewhat guilty watching our crew performing its maintenance chores: repairing soot blowers and welding new brackets for the TV and transmitting antennas. Forward, the deck gang is giving the second anchor chain a coat of paint. I overhear some griping, but feel little sympathy. The ABs are making fifteen dollars an hour in overtime (on weekends it's twenty) and will sit down tonight to a hand-carved rib roast. Tomorrow in port, if they want, they can blow it all on wine, women and shopping. What would they make of Dana's ship in 1834?

> All the running rigging has to be examined; chafing gear must be put on (mending the chafing gear alone would find constant employment for a man or two men, during working hours, for a whole voyage). . . . If we add to this all the tarring, greasing, oiling, varnishing, painting, scraping and scrubbing which is required in the course of a long voyage, and also remember this is all to be done in addition to watching at night, steering, reefing, furling, bracing, making and setting sail, and pulling, hauling, and climbing in every direction, one will hardly ask, "What can a sailor find to do at sea?"

The Captain was using this "free" day to work on must-do lists for two upcoming inspections. Every three years the U.S. Bureau of Shipping comes around to examine *Endurance*. Sea-Land needs its stamp of approval to get insurance. Then there's the annual Coast Guard inspection, with an in-depth one every other year. *This* is that year. The feeling is that without these agencies, American shipping companies would let their vessels slide. But the cost of upkeep, along with union pay scales and U.S. taxes, are driving American-flagged ships either into bankruptcy or into foreign flagging.

Foreign flagging was the way Aristotle Onassis began amassing his fortune. He registered his ships outside Greece, for cheaper labor, tax breaks and fewer regulations. After World War II, Liberia and Panama became popular registries for flags of convenience by offering non-resident shipowners low taxes, non-union labor and a policy called "Effective U.S. Control" (EUSC), which allows the U.S. to reclaim its commercial ships during wars or national emergencies.

Yet, there was always worry about the political instability in these countries. Enter the Marshall Islands, which has legal, financial and military ties to the U.S., no anti-American conflicts *and* is close, geographically, to the burgeoning Far East. A Hawaii-based businessman and fishing buddy of President Bush was able to cut through Defense Department red tape and arrange EUSC status for the Marshalls.

Sea-Land (which already had ships registered in Liberia, Panama, the Bahamas and Singapore) put three of *Endurance's* sisterships under Marshall Islands registry in 1994. That has the officers on *this* ship wondering about their futures. The American crews of those reflagged ships were dismissed in

Singapore and flown home to be replaced by Croatians and Filipinos. The Chief Mate and the Captain calculated that staffing each foreign-flag ship would cost the company only about $600,000 a year, while *Endurance's* permanent officers alone (two Captains, two Chief Engineers, two First Assistant Engineers and two Chief Mates) earn $1.4 million in salaries.

One of the ABs has worked up a cartoon on his computer, an unsubtle reference to *Endurance* falling into Micronesian hands. It shows a headhunter skipping around in a war mask, waving a spear. He's wearing a grass skirt and a Sea-Land cap. The cannibal has a resumé: five wives are listed under "Next of Kin" and he's the author of *Missionary Cuisine: How to Cook 'Em, How to Can 'Em.* The caption reads: "New Chief Mate, S/L *Endurance.*"

DECEMBER 13

Captain Harvey, perhaps over-cautious, gives "Golden Rock" a wide sweep while maneuvering Endurance *into Pusan Harbor. She's been assigned the space of a Russian ship, easing out. The two container ships, each with its pair of tugs, jockey about like sailboats rounding a mark, and no one on the bridge even breaks a sweat. The only actual sails in sight are those painted abstractly on two grain silos rising from a nearby terminal. The Captain comments, "You don't see Sunday sailors over here. Hard work and education — not recreation — that's what transformed modern Korea."*

As soon as the gangway goes down, up tramps a short middle-aged woman, with an egg-shaped body. She's wearing granny glasses and a crinkly smile. She reaches into the two black plastic bags she's lugged up to the 01 corridor and starts spreading fabrics and patterns against the wall.

"Oh, she makes custom suits?" I ask Bob. He grins. "Now she does. The rumor is that 'Sew-Sew,' as we call her, sold something else to the crew when she was in her prime."

Security is tight at the Pusan terminal. In Japan, we'd simply picked up our shore passes and walked off. Here, a shuttle bus waits on the dock with its motor running, to whisk sailors through a maze of trucks and containers to the security gate. Everybody is ordered to disembark and file through a shed staffed by grim guards in gray uniforms. After I pass through an airport-style scanner, a guard paws through my purse.

As usual, the Chief Mate has a strict time budget. We must be educated and recreated in three hours. Mr. Ryu, the Korean agent, writes out our destinations in his language. He advises that most of the local taxi drivers speak only a few words of English. Ours manages "America? . . . city . . . OK?" Lots of hand gestures, though — both hands — amid Manhattan-type traffic, hostile horn-honking, and grand prix sprints though twisting one-way streets.

Our first stop is a cemetery, ironically. The Captain had recommended we visit this United Nations Cemetery — a park really — where Korean War soldiers from countries like Turkey and Sweden lie in grassy plots. (Most of the U.S. dead were sent home for burial.) On this crisp bright morning, we feel decades removed from battle and miles away from responsibility. But the peace and quiet soon ends: suddenly the park is filled with hundreds of schoolchildren in dark blue uniforms. The boys are appropriately somber, but the girls — marching along in pairs, holding hands — can't stop giggling at Big Bob and the tall blonde alien.

Careening back to the city, Bob remarks, "Pusan has changed so much in just a couple of years. It used to be ramshackle, dirty, piles of rubble everywhere. Obviously there's been a big cleanup and building boom — just look at those slick shops. Let's walk from here."

We could be in London or Milan. Smart cafés serve mocha mousse and flavored coffees. Windows display Armani-style suits paired with long silvery scarves, and dresses with Parisian braiding. But only a block behind the glitsy thoroughfare lies the old Pusan that Bob remembers from a decade ago.

The International Market is a mile-square melange of exotic smells and sights. Oversized strawberries and scallions, split fish and pigs' heads ripening in the sun, kim chee (the spicy Korean version of sauerkraut) heaped in huge plastic pans, moped exhaust, musky leather from the stalls selling fake Gucci bags and genuine jackets, squid and octopus frying on gas stoves set on the sidewalk. The patrons squat down and eat out of the pans, saving on tables, chairs, and place settings.

Every material object on the planet seems to have been dumped at the market: rhinestone jewelry and real opals, Waterford goblets, stainless restaurant sinks, angora sweaters, copper wire, twisted medicinal roots, mink coats and polyester slacks, live shellfish sold by the scoopful, tents and backpacks, painted chopsticks, tires, blocks of seaweed the shape of doormats.

I want to get Bob a nice mug for his stale coffee, but finding this item becomes an exercise in frustration. In the cup/mug category, you could choose from plastic, tin, Corelle, glass, ceramic, paper-thin china. We uncover thousands, jumbled in piles between notepads and cosmetic brushes; half-buried under lace tablecloths; neatly boxed in sets. Some with matching lids, painted with English flowers or Miró designs from France. After two hours we discover IT: a Korean original with four cartoon cats calling "Miaou Miaou Miaou" and one tiny fish inside the rim.

Bob's time is up . . . the four o'clock watch again. He hails another taxi and hands the driver a slip of paper spelling "Texas Street" in Korean. "I'll drop you off there," Bob states, "And show you where to catch the bus back to the ship. Don't worry about getting lost; I'm sure you'll bump into half the crew."

Sun Myung Moon was born on the infamous Texas Street, but that's not why seamen beat a path to it. It used to be one of Pusan's famous red-light districts, though it changed character when South Korea's economy did. Now, most of Texas Street's females sell leather goods, watches and athletic shoes instead of themselves.

"Buy yourself some shoes and whatever else catches your eye," Bob says as he hands me half-a-dozen bills of 10,000 won, the Korean currency. (At 770 won to the dollar, I wasn't as rich as I looked.) Vince the AB had given me essential instructions: "You never know if the 'Reeboks' are seconds or knock-offs. First, you have to try them on — both feet. Then look hard at where the sole is glued on; I've had some pull apart after the first day."

It takes some searching, but I find three pair that fit and wear their glue proudly. They add up to 23,100 won, or $30. After that, I wander around, curious to catch a glimpse of the bad old days. There are still a few bars that look seedy enough to satisfy a China Coaster. A pouty "bar girl" in a crotch-high leather skirt and slingback heels stands smoking outside a dark doorway under a sign reading "Ocean Room" and throws me a cold stare. I'm intruding in her territory, like coming eye to eye with a shark patrolling its reef.

As I start back toward the shuttle bus I have the eerie feeling of being followed. I turn around to find four husky drunks behind me. They start catcalling in what I suppose is Russian; then two of them stagger up, closing in on me. The other two run in front of and encircle me, laughing and hooting. I can feel my face flush and my heart pound. Then I spot George the electrician in the road ahead — George who looks like Popeye with his shiny bald head but is Lancelot at this moment. He gives me the courage to make an end run around my tormentors.

Is old George's crusty voice just a touch soft when he says, "Ya gotta be real, real careful out here . . . lotsa bad shit goin' on"? On the bus ride back, he gives me an earful on the "Ruskies," whose fishing boats stop in Pusan to resupply. "The bastards have taken over Texas Street and driven all the prices up . . . next thing y'know they'll be grabbin' our jobs!"

Back in my room, I flop on the bed and close my eyes. All I want to do is stay here in my nest, but Bob has made a date. For some time, Mr. Ryu has been asking the Chief Mate out for an "authentic Korean meal." Bob has always begged off because he's not big on fish with intact appendages, and he's heard that Koreans eat d-o-g and, God forbid, even c-a-t. Since I — the adventurous diner — will be along, he figures I can distract Mr. R. while he picks through his food.

Mr. Ryu is waiting in Bob's office when the Chief Mate gets off watch. He reminds me of a middle-aged cherub, soft and spongy, with an angelic smile. He tells me proudly that he converted from Buddhism to Christianity some twenty years ago. I would follow him anywhere and we do — down into a subway. Mr. Ryu proudly walks us through a subterannean city of bright boutiques, marble pillars and mosaics of ships sailing in jagged glass seas. There's even a Samsung TV mounted above each track to amuse the weary commuter.

The subway cars are clean, fast, and so crammed — even after rush hour — that we have to strap-hang. Except for their Asian faces, the passengers could be from urban-anywhere: men in black suits, teens in jeans, mothers with sleepy children and shopping bags, all with that universal glaze of the subway rider.

We exit at the fourth stop and follow our leader up a steep stairway that empties into a dark street. The only signs of life are trash bags piled on the cobblestones. Down a few blocks, suddenly lights shimmer like an oasis above dark wooden doors with dragon carvings. The doors of the restaurant Mr. Ryu has chosen open into fantasyland, where, on the main level, tables sit on a transparent floor with scarlet carp swimming beneath diners' feet. A six-foot chandelier shaped like an inverted wedding cake shoots sparklers over the glass surfaces.

A waiter in a white karate-style uniform leads us up to the second floor. At the top of the stairs, Mr. Ryu slips out of his shoes, and so do we, examining our socks for holes or worse. We pad after a young woman in a red kimono to a low rosewood table and settle onto batik cushions, trying to arrange our long American legs. At least my feet are happy, rubbing over the heat which radiates from the wooden floor.

Several sips into a Dry Crown beer, a silver cauldron of fish soup with tofu and scallions arrives. A few swallows later, more kimonos and a procession of plates, a dozen dishes in all, each one edible art. Slices of raw fish, draped over sculpted cucumbers; prawns arranged in a circle, tentacles touching; marble-size meatballs on a bed of glazed carrots; fans and flowers of marinated veggies. Nothing that resembles a household pet. We follow Mr. Ryu's example and tear apart the designs with silver chopsticks.

Just as I'm feeling wonderfully mellow, a pyramid of tempura shrimp, king crab, green beans and sweet potatoes appears. The potatoes are as crunchy as candy — a perfect way to end the meal. But no. Red Kimono pushes plates aside and plunks down another course: four varieties of kim chee (cucumber, cabbage, radish, and seaweed) and a whole steamed fish. And after that: individual casseroles of rice and beans, with several sauces to ladle on for extra abundance.

Bob stopped eating an hour ago, but determined not to offend — and relentlessly urged on by our host — I stab away blindly. The meal has become an athletic event, except the finish line keeps moving. Finally, we all receive a fingerbowl of sudsy liquid. I sigh and get ready to dip my fingers when Mr. Ryu lifts his bowl to his lips. "Sweet rice water . . . very good for digestion . . . you drink," he commands.

DECEMBER 14

After a miserable night of indigestion, I'm still in major pain: the worst food hangover ever. If I smell something cooking, I'll be sick. So while Bob goes down to breakfast, I walk out on deck to get some air. Big mistake. An acrid smog has settled over the city. The harbor is redolent of sewage and kim chee. I look down, remembering a passage from Daphne du Maurier about a timeless waste of seaweed tresses. I wish this "timeless stuff" in the water was half as romantic: splintered boards, rotten mango skins and yellowed plastic bottles rub against the hull. That does it. I race for the head and throw up Mr. Ryu's glorious meal.

A Mexican containership is waiting for our dock space. After twenty-four hours in Pusan, Endurance is engaged in another ship-shuffle. She's listing to port, which makes me even woozier, but I can take to my bed while the other debauchers must go back to work. And I can rest easy that Ken escaped Korea with his virtue intact, in spite of the rumor that the ABs were going to "get him laid." He brought in two brown leather jackets to show Bob and me, saying proudly, "Wow! I can't believe the bargains!"

I lie down with a kaleidoscope of images tumbling through my head: leather and garbage, Gucci and gravestones, painted silos and rice water. It's all too much to take in on one day. I give up, and spiral into sleep.

Chapter 17

CROSSING THE EAST CHINA SEA, ENROUTE TO OKINAWA

DECEMBER 16

Endurance has made her way through the Korea Strait into the East China Sea. Enroute, she crossed the 30° latitude line, which greatly pleases the Chief Mate. "Below 30 is where you want to be this time of year. It's a whole different world, sunny and balmy, when Korea is usually bitter cold," he explains.

He's right: as we approach the island of Okinawa, the air turns seductively warm. Tropical islands with curving palms and white-sand beaches appear at first to be fantasies of a starved sailor who has been too long deprived of sun, clear water and blue skies. But if I'm hallucinating so is Bob's guidebook, which promises shelling, diving and windsurfing around snug little coves.

Okinawa, a 463 square-mile island, has drawn Chinese, Mongolians, Koreans, Japanese and Filipinos over the centuries. They came to fish and farm; sweet potatoes and sugar cane took to the island's soil. It's hard to imagine red blood mixing with these turquoise waters — but 12,500 U.S. servicemen and 110,000 Japanese were slaughtered in the infamous 1945 battle during World War II. Although the island belongs to Japan, there are still about 25,000 American troops stationed here. Every year the American government compels Sea-Land and American President Lines to bid against each other for the contract to supply the military bases.

Sea-Land won this round and will be dropping off turkeys and ice cream for the soldiers' Christmas dinners. Although the Chief Mate should feel a touch of patriotic pride that he's kept the poultry at 0° and ice cream at −15°, his brain is always too busy for such emotions. Another container has everyone's attention: it's listed on the manifest as "Chocolate-Covered Macadamia Nuts." If only some Act-of-God would cut the seal, a six-inch metal strip fitted over a hasp.

For the first time since leaving Florida, I'm standing outside in a T-shirt, my torso soaking up vitamin D. As it shallows, the water changes from flat Williamsburg blue to shimmering sapphire. And it stays pure all the way into the harbor: no sewage or garbage breaks the surface. Twin tugs chug out to guide Endurance past a long breakwater to port, bent like an elbow's crook. The tugboats are dressed to kill with electric blue hulls, military green decks, white "houses" and orange masts aft.

To starboard, a JAL jet with its scarlet rising-sun logo drops onto a runway at the water's edge. To the left of the airport sits the capital city of Naha. Most of the buildings are painted white, with a few pastel hues. They seem to be tossed haphazardly on low hills; an occasional skyscraper leaps from the jumble. A high bridge arches like an eyebrow, drawing attention to a bay below and the medley of fishing boats it protects.

We come in ahead of an unusual vessel called The Performer, *with a sign on its house declaring its business:* "Oceaneering." *It has a rusty red hull, tall orange superstructure, and helicopter pad on the foredeck.* Endurance *is backing into the dock — a feat I never would have thought possible. The tugs pull and push, roll out and wind up their tow lines from hydraulically controlled reels. Part of this maneuver is still done by "feel": the C/M on the bow radios up to the Captain, "If you come in straight, you'll clear the bow of* The Performer *by fifteen feet."*

After the tugs nudge Endurance *into the dock, I sense something is missing. It takes me a few minutes to realize that no giant container cranes are maneuvering along railroad-type tracks to pick off the cargo. Instead, a few of the old portable variety lumber across the tarmac of the quay on their own treads. Fork-lift trucks scoot a mosaic of purple, green and red containers about in all directions. The scene looks like child's play with Tinker Toys, compared to the high-tech operations in Oakland, Japan, and Korea.*

I'm as high as humanly possible on a dry ship. First, the lush climate and now a batch of letters from home! I'd chosen Okinawa as a mail-drop because I figured if Sea-Land could get supplies to the troops, they could locate me. I tear open an envelope from my son Jeff, relieved to hear that he, his wife Diane, four mongrel cats, one pedigreed Coon, a white poodle and the goldfish are fine. Jeff also writes, "Mom, guess what? You and I may have more in common than you think. We [Patrick Air Force Base in Florida, where he coordinates a computer network] are sending up a communications satellite next week. I believe the INMARSAT system is what you guys use on the ship." Awesome, *as Jeff himself would say. I must check it out with Keith.*

A manila packet from Becky — my best-buddy who married us (as a notary public) and agreed to house-sit while I went seafaring — holds a few bills, news from other friends, and this about my cat: "I'm afraid

Daphne's getting fat; she's discovered fish dip and Triskets." I'm happy, sad, and homesick all at the same time. *I finally understand the significance of written words from loved ones, a world away.*

I had letters of my own to send, but no one could leave until after the fire-and-boat drill. Unlike some ships, *Endurance* is squeaky clean on safety. Once a week, the fire bell (officially known as the "general alarm") rings a staccato signal: seven short blasts followed by a long one. On alternate weeks from the safety films, the entire crew, except for the Captain and the quartermaster, who stay on the bridge, assembles by the two lifeboats on the embarkation deck.

I've been assigned to the port one, which nests outside the messroom. It gives me pause because two of my fellow castaways would be the Chief Mate and Louis the Steward. The former regularly sneaks french fries from my plate; the latter would surely throw me to the sharks for a scrap of beef jerky.

Normally, the boats are lowered several feet — just enough to test their mechanisms — but this is to be the once-a-quarter occasion to drop the boats into the water. Bob puts Frank, the Second Mate, in charge of a lifeboat crew who will take it out under engine power, then row it back. Frank cajoles six volunteers who look about as enthusiastic as Bligh's mutineers.

I like the permanently wry expression Frank wears on his craggy face. At coffee break while Bob and the Captain gossip about their Merchant Marine cronies, Frank and I have progressed to other things. He told me he graduated from Vermont's Goddard College ("the only place for a misfit like me") and then moved to California, where he slipped easily into a lifestyle of Esalen, EST, hypnosis, and recovery programs. He's given me old copies of "The New Yorker" and "Harper's." Frank, like Bob, is on this ship for one reason only: to finance fun ashore. The Second Mate's jobs on the ship — in charge of the stern during docking, standing the 12 to 4 watches, taking responsibility for the charts by correcting and stowing them and laying out courses — offer him no challenges, which fuels his cynicism. "Being out here really messes up my head, so I hide out in my mountain cabin when I get off."

Frank fixes his sarcastic eye on the lifeboat drill. "My lifelong dream: Captain of the Goddard Rowing Team!" However, the Team can't get the boat to budge from its davits. After much tugging, swearing and consulting, George the electrician takes a hammer to one of the frozen-with-rust pelican hooks, whose purpose is to hold the boat alongside so the crew can clamber aboard. It takes more than five minutes to free the hook. Well, at least we're not the Titanic.

As the boat is lowered by its wire cables, three knotted manropes uncoil. Their upper ends are fastened to a cable called a "jackstay" strung across the davits. They provide emergency hand-holds for the lifeboat crew to grab onto if the boat falls. The ropes must be thrown clear once the boat hits the water, so they don't get caught on anyone or anything, especially the propeller, when the boat starts up. But something goes wrong. When the engineer tries the engine, it coughs out a cloud of exhaust, then the lifeboat leaps ahead. Two of the crew scramble to free themselves from the manropes. The Chief Mate, watching from the railing, yells down, "That was really stupid. Someone could have broken a fucking leg!"

The lifeboat putt-putts away, then turns around and wobbles back uncertainly under oar power. The oars are simply a refresher in rowing, which is recorded in the log book as "crew exercised under oars." After the lifeboat is raised back up, the off-duty crew is finally let loose, like kids at recess. Bob, hyper from the near-accident, peels off his life preserver and Sea-Land cap and urges me, "Get ready to take off."

As we walk toward the gangway with our bikes, we run into Keith, who announces his day will be spent at the Seaman's Club. Specifically the bar. "But I always visit The Wall first; have you guys seen it?" he asks. We leave the bikes (unlocked) and stroll with Keith to the breakwater that wraps around one of Naha's inner harbors.

The breakwater wall is constructed of four-foot high slabs of concrete; graffiti artists use the shoreward side for murals. On one, an abstraction in the style of Stuart Davis weaves in the words "LASTFLOWER," "FRIENDWAVE," and "LOVEPEACE." On another, Sammy Davis, Jr., in caricature, grins at the liquor bottle he holds up. Further along, a blue Keith Haring figure boogies through a field of red poppies. And a discreet mermaid (no nipples) lounges in a pool of water, beneath gold stars shooting across a black sky.

There is little obscenity; the word "SEX" is scrawled once, in foot-high scarlet letters. On this half-mile long public wall, written sentiments tend to be sentimental, such as "We Are Lovers. We have been in LOVE with each other. Wataru & Kumiko." One displays a heartfelt message of another sort: "FRIENDS DON'T LET FRIENDS RE-ENLIST." Peeling paint gives the older murals the appearance of classical frescoes.

Enroute to the Seaman's Club on Captain Harvey's three-speed bike, Bob forges ahead on his ten-speed. The only route is straight up and then down a dauntingly high bridge, with four lanes of ferocious traffic. As Bob disappears over the summit, I slowly make it to the top, then plunge down, wobbling in terror. A truck nearly sideswipes me; the bike bounces off the curb, and I crash into the oncoming traffic.

I lie there stunned and crying as cars, trucks, motorcycles roar by unconcerned, as if a foreign female lying in their path were an entirely normal event. When I finally pick myself up and stagger down the rest of the bridge slope, I find Bob frowning. He says to me, "I hope you didn't break the Captain's bike."

On the ensuing slow, sulky ride to the Seaman's Club, we pedal silently past mossy hillside tombs — some dating from the 1400s — carved atop each other, condos for the dead. On the harbor opposite Endurance's dock, a public swimming pool meanders around palm trees and fountains, elegant as a four-star resort. My aching body would much prefer to be there, floating in the water.

The Bud that flows from the Seaman's Club tap takes some of the sting out of the day. Then I spot Ken the cadet at the other end of the bar, hunched over, pen to postcard, a golden mug in front of him, too!

"Hi there, Ken, can I buy you another beer?"

"Well thank you, Ma'am. Sure appreciate it. I'm drinking ginger ale, though."

On the way back to the ship, we're an unhealthy contrast: the C/M and I panting through the sticky heat, up and over that bloody bridge again, with Ken jogging alongside, barely breaking a sweat.

By the time we arrive at Endurance, I've worked through most of my physical and emotional bruises. Before I can savor Bob's delayed apology, Frank strides over to announce, "The Captain wants to see you in his office; we have a big problem."

Clark, one of the deck ABs, had come back to the ship in a taxi. Accompanying him were eight cases of Budweiser. To add to his blatant behavior, he lifted the cases onto *Endurance* with the ship's small crane (which is used to hoist provisions and other stores aboard). As Clark's misfortune would have it, the Captain was walking toward the gangway at that very moment.

With the Chief Mate as a witness, the Captain wrote up a glum Clark in the official logbook, then told him to pack his duffel bag and find his own way home. Clark got paid off for his three weeks' work: $1,600. But the plane ticket to San Francisco cost $1,400, and with what he had to pay for his Okinawa hotel room, not to mention the beer and the taxi, I was not alone in having a bad day.

Clark implicated two other ABs, but they denied involvement. Some quick math showed that with three weeks left to go, Clark would have had to go through nine beers a day to finish the eight cases himself. The Captain could have probed deeper, but to fly *three* replacement seamen out to the Far East would have delivered a TKO to the company treasurer. He let it go.

Alcohol used to be part of shipboard life. Many ships' owners were alcoholics; they'd take a bottle to the captain's quarters and afterwards stagger down the gangway, waving good-bye to their drunken captain. Until recently, alcohol was still tolerated aboard some ships but after several transportation accidents, including the *Exxon Valdez* incident, safety policies were rewritten and now senior ships' officers are assumed to *always* be on duty.

Though Sea-Land runs dry ships, one of their competitors handles drinking this way: you can buy beer at the ship's bar; other beverages consumed in the rooms are tolerated but not publicly encouraged. However, a crewmember can't walk more than a few feet without seeing a warning that a blood alcohol level of more than .04 — within four hours of his watch time — is cause for immediate dismissal.

One case has given the crew hours of pleasure. An abusive Captain was giving a soft-spoken Second Mate a terrible time one entire voyage. The Mate took it without a word, but when the ship docked in the U.S., he got his revenge. The Captain went ashore and came back drunk. Waiting for him at the gangway was the Second Mate, who had called the Coast Guard. The Captain was declared unfit for duty and fired.

Endurance eases out of Naha Harbor at twilight; I stand at the rail of the bridge-wing just like a tourist. As the sun drops below the horizon, it drags the heat with it. The rosy air is soft as a lover's touch. The bridge I battled looks like a cobweb strung across the face of the city. As we glide past the airport, runway lights cast diamond, ruby, and sapphire reflections onto the water.

I'm still standing there, seduced by the tropical breeze and transfixed by the starry night, when Bob materializes at my elbow. Perhaps still trying to make up, he says softly, "Have I ever told you about my passion for celestial navigation? It started when I was a young cadet. I felt I was following in the footsteps of Captain Cook and his protégé Bligh when I took the noon sight with my sextant and chronometer.

"Celestial navigation is a satisfying melding of science and art. For the noon sight, the navigator tracks the sun through the sextant as it reaches a point either due north or due south. This is its highest altitude of the day, at which point it's hovering directly over the vessel's meridian of longitude. During the few minutes before this moment (known as "local apparent noon" or LAN), he slowly turns the micrometer drum (on modern sextants) or the thumb screw (on the more antique instruments) in the direction of increasing altitude. The very bottom of the sun's fiery rim, as seen through the telescope, is adjusted so that it just kisses the horizon.

"But today," Bob ends ruefully, "with the arrival of the GPS, navigation is a no-brainer. It's as easy as taking latitude and longitude figures off a screen."

We stand together under the stars, each lost in our own fantasies. Bob pictures Captain Cook on the poop deck of his Royal Navy ship, shooting the sun with self-assurance in a ritual that appeared to be magic to the uninitiated. I imagine a gentle romantic era when there were no Captain's bikes, no clumsy females, and no short-tempered Chief Mates.

DECEMBER 17, THE NEXT MORNING

Who would have thought that eight cases of beer would take on the dimensions of a tragedy, but that's how it feels when Bob comes back from his watch and announces, "They're history. Had to toss them overboard myself. Captain's orders." Since the Chief Mate should set an example by being morally and environmentally correct, he waited until Endurance *was twenty-five miles away from land.*

"You didn't even save a couple of cans for us?" I whine.

Chapter 18

ENTERING THE TAIWAN STRAITS

DECEMBER 18

Endurance steams along a chain of islands called the Ryukus toward Taiwan, which used to be called Formosa ("Beautiful Island") during the five decades it was occupied by the Japanese before World War II. Two hundred forty miles long, just a hundred miles of water separates it from the People's Republic of China, which, believing that *it* owns the island, not the Nationalist Chinese, regularly makes threats to take it over.

When *Endurance* rounds the southern tip of Taiwan to reach the port of Kaohsiung on the western side, she enters the Taiwan Straits. All seems quiet, the seas as well as the skies. The air is still pleasantly warm for winter. I've noted from the chart that we're just south of the Tropic of Cancer, where the "Torrid Zone" begins, extending all the way to the Tropic of Capricorn south of the equator.

On the bridge, I find Vince and Ken cracking up. The Chief Mate is chanting "Na-me-yo-ho-rengay-keyo" into the VHF's mike. He says with his bad-little-boy grin, "I once went to a cult meeting in the Village, and I've always remembered their chant. First, it drives the guys on the boats nuts, then they join in until everyone's chanting. But I've got to get serious. We're entering an area of wooden fishing boats which our radar can't pick up. I just pray I make it to retirement without sinking one of them; many are home to large families."

I can see why Bob is so uptight. Near the harbor entrance, the small fishing boats — looking dangerously unstable with their high poop decks, similar to those on Columbus' ships — meander across Endurance's path, as if they had never heard of privileged or burdened vessels. The tugs that guide us in look similarly haphazard: rusty and unkempt. The crew wears sweatbands rather than hard hats, and dirty overalls instead of uniforms. The shipshape Japanese would be horrified.

Still, I am excited. Another country and a new port with an exotic name, Kaohsiung. It's pronounced "cow-shung," although I've heard a few of the crew call it "cow-dung," referring to its pollution and general decrepitude. Indeed, hovering clouds turn out to be smog, stinging my eyes when we turn into the channel. A raggedy band of Taiwanese waiting on the dock all sport surgical masks.

Bob tells me, "These are the Kaohsiung paint gangs, marine cosmeticians who camouflage the ship's age spots before sending her out again. They may be on the shabby side, but they're good workers. One time when Endurance's letters needed painting, not one of our ABs had the guts to man a scaffold dangling from the bow. So along comes this tiny Taiwanese lady, about seventy years old, with a bowline around her ankle. She gets the job done in about five minutes."

When I return to the office, I find a fellow in white coveralls standing by the Chief Mate's desk. Bob introduces him as "Jimmy, the paint gang boss." Then he asks me, "Don't you think he resembles John Wayne?" It's *amazing: Jimmy — a short wiry Taiwanese — has the same squinty eyes, thin lips and long furrowed face as The Duke. He also has something our hero lacked: teeth rimmed in silver, which sparkle when he smiles.*

"Look what Jimmy brought us," Bob says, lifting up two plastic supermarket bags. They're crammed full of lichee nuts, persimmons, tanger-ines, and pear-apples — so enormous, I'm suspicious of human fertilizer. Bob continues, "Since I'm the one who arranges for the ship's painting, Jimmy brings me baksheesh. Now for the gift that will make you cry." There, on the floor inside our stateroom, sits an entire case of Taiwan Beer, soon to join its buddies on the ocean floor.

Keith extends an invitation. "I know the Chief Mate is always busy. Want to help me pick out some videos?" This is an honor: to be half-entrusted with the movie fund. And I could use some diversion from Polish Politics in Transition *and* Psycho Nutrition, *which I checked out of the crew's library.*

When I meet Keith at the gangway, he reports, "Vince is buddies with this taxi driver and says we can ride with him." Grateful for any transportation other than a bicycle, I wave at Vince down below in a grimy compact car, its horn blowing.

Like the fishermen in the channel, Kaohsiung drivers follow no rules of the road. Stop signs, red lights, centerlines, intersections . . . who cares? I cower behind a tourist map which informs me that the city has a population of 1.4 million; it is Taiwan's primary industrial center, as well as a vital seaport in northeast Asia. Meanwhile, Fong the driver leans on the horn and demonstrates pin-point skill at squeezing his vehicle into the smallest possible space at the highest possible speed.

At the same time, Fong tries to exchange his NT (the Taiwan currency) for our dollars, talks up his family's gift shop, bargains for the square white sapphire on Vince's pinkie finger. "Sorry, Fong," Vince vigorously shakes his head. "Michiko would murder me. It's her old engagement ring."

After a blur of indistinguishable buildings, covered with vertical banners with Chinese characters, and a million motorbikes on both roads and sidewalks, we finally escape from Fong's taxi. The first thing we meet is a caged monkey suspended from a tree. He reaches down for a handout and bares his teeth when we come up empty. Beyond the tree, which has taken root through a crack in the sidewalk, is a joint calling itself the "Starlight Room." Not a star in sight when I glance in; instead, the interior seems as black and forbidding as a pharaoh's tomb. "Welcome to 'The Combat Zone,' " Keith announces. Every day ashore with the crew is another initiation into the sailor's milieu of sex and bargains.

"So, this is Taiwan's Texas Street?"

"Yep, but the only deals here are knock-off Rolexes and pirated films. We used to get some authentic stuff off scrapped ships — like old bronze lamps and portholes — but now that's all fake too. You said you wanted some watches, so we'll do that first."

Bob's instructions: "Go see Judy at the bookstore; get yourself a nice watch and a gold 'Rolex' for our next door neighbor; I promised him one." Keith points me toward a sign that says simply BOOKS, a few doors down from The Starlight Room.

An Asian woman about my age helps me choose a guidebook. I ask her, "Is there a Judy around here?" "I'm Judy," she says, as if she knows she doesn't look the part. She seems suspicious about me too, silently sizing me up, when I ask to see some watches. But when I describe Bob ("He comes here on his ship several times a year. He's that really big guy with the little space between his teeth"), she makes the connection. "Okay," she says, a little reluctantly, "Come with me."

After navigating a dark corridor, I follow Judy into a darker kitchen where a scarred wood table holds remnants of breakfast. Judy takes the rice bowls, drops them in the sink and replaces them with two leather attaché cases that she lifted from a drawer. When she opens the cases, gold glimmers in the dim light. Even if it's fool's gold, the contrast with the dingy room is startling.

I treat myself to a "Cartier" because it has a nautical rope motif around the face. Paul's watch could be the real thing, except the second hand ticks, rather than sweeps, along. But for twenty-five bucks U.S., it seems like such a deal. If the watches stop ticking tomorrow, I'll feel I got my money's worth. The flush of excitement, participating in back-room Asian intrigue, is equal to the price.

Armed with the Movie Fund, Keith and I try our luck at the video store. Taiwan may have perfected piratic copying, but the buying part remains oddly low-tech. A gaunt old man pushes several photo albums across the counter. On each page, half a dozen movie labels, the size on wine bottles, lie under plastic protectors. Each has a number scrawled in Magic Marker beside it.

We have enough cash for eight movies, but the elves out back hadn't copied any of the titles on our wish list. So we flip through the albums, trying to find something new for the blood-thirsty aboard (action), the space cadets (sci-fi), the old-timers (war or westerns), the airheads (slapstick). The old fellow behind the counter, noting our dilemma, believes he has the solution. He plunks down another notebook. "Sex," he pronounces, grinning.

Keith shakes his head. "Forget it. Any blue film that finds its way into our video library is history by the next day. Even 9½ Weeks and Wild Orchid have disappeared."

We settle on Spartacus, a Roger Moore James Bond, one Woody Allen, two Steven Seagal, and Grumpy Old Men. I reflect that more than one of the crew will relate to that title.

After three beers with Keith and Vince at the Seaman's Club and another Fong road race back to the ship, I giggle all through dinner, waving my new watch at Bob. He gets serious. "I've been thinking. I don't know if it's such a good idea your going off drinking with the crew. I feel pretty rested; why don't I skip my nap tomorrow and we can bike into town."

At the expression on my face, he retracts. "Okay, okay, there's a local fellow — the entrepreneur who supplies the painting gangs. I think he can take us on a tour."

"Great, as long as his name isn't Fong."

DECEMBER 19, NEXT MORNING

A whole day with my husband, a magic-carpet ride away from the ship and into the country! The "carpet" is an immaculate gold Toyota, with Johnson, a diminutive Taiwanese, at the wheel.

The gold brocade seat covers with ruffles on the edges aren't your everyday auto decor. Johnson sees me run my hand over them and comments, "This car was made in United States. No Japanese imports allowed in Taiwan." The Taiwanese are respectful of American attempts to correct the imbalance of trade; one of their methods is to import Toyotas from the U.S. instead of Japan.

Johnson, a blessedly careful driver, maneuvers us out of the city and into farm country, with small settlements every few miles. Rows of banana trees are tidily planted and tenderly maintained; a blue plastic bag encases each stalk, to protect them from bugs and blemishes. Away from the city smog, my eyes clear up — and the colors of the countryside sharpen, as if I'd put on polarized glasses.

I've been flipping through my new Taiwan guidebook. Along with the usual sights and restaurants, there's a chapter on "Issues." Yes, the book admits, "Air pollution is out of control — but overcrowding in the cities is a matter of choice. We don't like to live in the country. It's too lonely. That's *why Americans keep pets." And about child prostitution: "Mothers who've grown too old for the profession sell their children. The practice is supported by Japanese businessmen."*

Suddenly, around a bend in the road, a misty green mountain fills the sky, as ethereal as a Chinese watercolor. A gargantuan gold Buddha sits cross-legged on the summit. Below him some sort of complex is scattered around the mountainside. "Fo Kuang Shan Buddhist Center," proclaims Johnson with pride. "First we visit museum." Now that's usually a magic word for me, but I find this one . . . how else can I say it? . . . a one-note theme: ivory Buddhas, stone Buddhas, crystal Buddhas, amber Buddhas, jade Buddhas, even fabric Buddhas. Johnson seems entranced. Respecting his beliefs, I don't say anything negative. However, I do poke Bob to pick up the pace.

The next building fills us in on Chinese history we were never taught. One glass-enclosed exhibit depicts how the primitive plow evolved, to keep pace with China's burgeoning peasantry. I'm awed by a mechanical wooden cow, tall as a tree. Like the Trojan horse, it was rolled to faraway battlefields — a camouflaged armory filled with firearms for the soldiers.

Meanwhile, we've picked up an entourage of teenage novitiates. With shaved heads and long black robes, their sex is questionable. At first I'm convinced they're boys. But when one of them gets the courage to speak: ("Welcome." "American?" "You like?") it's with a high soprano. "What should we call them . . . the Monkettes?" Bob whispers.

What an advantage to having a local drive you around, making all the decisions. Johnson's next stopover was a hotel. Not any hotel, but "The Grand Hotel," built by Madame Chiang Kai-shek, now about 95 years old and living in the United States. It's almost as if her late husband, "The Generalissimo," were still around; monuments to him dotted our route. In 1949, Chiang Kai-shek fled the mainland for Taiwan when Chairman Mao established the People's Republic of China. He brought with him Mei-ling Soong, his fourth wife (#2 and #3 were Shanghai prostitutes), two sons, 800,000 troops and two million followers.

The Generalissimo's power in Taiwan was absolute and brutal. Thirty thousand opponents, mostly native Taiwanese, were massacred by his army. However, he had taken all the gold from the mainland treasury and used this to establish a flourishing capitalistic society. By the early 1950s, Taiwan's economic growth had given its population the highest standard of living in Asia, except for Japan's.

Meanwhile, Madame Chiang, who craved power and wealth, designed her Grand Hotel to look like a temple, with red latticework and a pagoda-style roof of gold. Befitting one who demanded that her silk sheets be changed every time her body touched them, the hotel exuded an old-fashioned opulence. We had a small sample of it: satiny mango ice cream in the paneled coffee shop.

Finally, Johnson hustles us inside a small restaurant featuring long glass cases of squid, octopus and shrimp on ice. Schools of fish swim in tanks of bubbling water. Soon after we're seated, food begins arriving bit by bit: marinated fava beans and okra, a kale-type vegetable in dark gravy, whole baby squid, slivers of cabbage over shaved ice with a pink dip, something that looks like french fries, except they have fins. And heads. And tails. After an appetizer of fish-fries, I pick up a plump squid in my chopsticks and pop the cephalopod in my mouth. Bob watches with disbelief. "Yummy," I pronounce, "Except for the eyeballs."

On the way back to the ship, Johnson asks a favor: "Okay to pick up wife and kids?" His cellular phone produces his family, waiting in front of a cold stone building, an unmistakable "School" in any culture. A stylish woman in a navy blue suit introduces herself as, "Terry, and this is Davey and Jenny. She's five and he's seven." She said she had come into town for a political meeting. "There's an election soon. We take the vote seriously because we always worry about mainland China."

The Johnsons are like a middle-class family from Anywhere; that is, until Terry fiddles in her purse, pulls out a three-inch squid and hands it to Jenny. At first, I think it's a cute toy. Jenny rolls it around in her hands for a few minutes, then begins nibbling on the tentacles. "Crunch, crunch, crunch," then the whole head disappears into the little mouth. I am no longer top dog when it comes to consuming weird and wonderful Chinese cuisine.

Following the Chief Mate up the gangway to the stairwell, I have to step over a dozen or so bodies lying in the corridor, still as stone. "Has there been an epidemic?" I wonder. "No," he laughs. "They're longshoremen. Not all the men in a gang are required on deck, so they just flop down anywhere and nap."

Once again, Endurance prepares to cast off. The "Single Up" order has been given, and three tension wires at each end of the ship have been winched back on board. Two Taiwanese stand ready to cast off the remaining polypropylene lines, which our deck hands have slackened. The engine, warming up for the past hour, will resume its reassuring Thump, Trump, Thump any second now.

A diffuse golden glow encircles the ship; it's the late afternoon light, commingled with smog. I take my camera out on deck to capture the curious atmosphere. A black steel crane fills the viewfinder. Its work completed, the gantry has folded itself up so the ship can clear it when backing out. Backlighted against the molten sky, the crane's legs and "neck" look like a futuristic giraffe. I snap the shutter and freeze it in time.

Chapter 19

APPROACHING HONG KONG

DECEMBER 20

Can our ship, like the Ancient Mariner's, be haunted? One of Endurance's seamen is either "possessed" — or faking it so he can go home.

Irwin is the AB who stands the 8 to 12 watch with Bill the Third Mate. They're a Mutt-and-Jeff pair: the AB towering over his officer by about a foot. He's also on the solemn side, which plays off against Bill's nicotine nervousness. Despite their differences — or maybe because of them — the nautical odd couple drifts calmly through their eight hours a day together.

Several days ago Irwin got upset at the C/M's AB, Vince, for some offhand remark the latter made when the two changed watches. Actually it was only Vince's tone that offended Irwin, as the Third Mate discovered when he played referee. Everything seemed back to normal until two days ago, when Irwin complained of stomach cramps on watch: "I don't feel so good; I think someone's poisoned the drinking water and maybe the food too."

From there, things went downhill and the Third Mate presented the Chief Mate with Irwin's list of laments:

- "The Captain snuck in my room and shined a red light in my eyes.
- Fluid is seeping out of my feet.
- There's a camera on the ceiling watching me.
- I can feel a tumor taking over my stomach.
- It's hard to breathe, but if I open the porthole the spies will come in."

The C/M, who had his share of paranoid personalities when he practiced psychology, pulled out Irwin's medical form. The AB had listed one prescription he was taking for high blood pressure. However, the C/M wondered whether Irwin was neglecting to take some psychotropic medication, and decided to search his room. He found no drugs at all — legal or otherwise.

The Chief Mate (wearing the "Medical Officer" hat) must report every illness/injury to the Sea-Land Medical Claim Department when the ship returns to the States. After examining the patient, he wrote the following:

> Irwin W's paranoid ideation, his extreme agitation, and his irrational perception of his own body functions are indicative of an acute paranoid episode. A diagnosis of paranoid schizophrenia must be held in abeyance, pending more information on his psychiatric history. He is a Vietnam veteran (a draftee) so at one time in his adult life at least, he was functioning at a normal level with

ego strength adequate to withstand the stresses of military life.

I believe that Mr. W., in his present condition, cannot function in his capacity as AB aboard the Sea-Land *Endurance*. He probably requires psychological testing and long-term observation before a proper psychiatric diagnosis can be made. Of course it is entirely feasible that this current paranoid episode is the result of some discrete physical dysfunction.

The Chief Mate called Irwin to his office, to sign the medical log. At the time I was sitting at my computer, pretending to type, but of course eavesdropping. When the C/M excused himself for a few minutes to confer with the Captain, I stole a good look at the AB. If Irwin was faking his illness, he was an actor of Academy Award caliber. His shoulders and mouth drooped; his watery eyes were rimmed in red. He'd locked his hands across his belly, as if to hold the demons in.

The office phone rang. It was the C/M. "Nancy, don't say anything. Just go in the bedroom *right now* and *lock yourself in*. The Captain said he heard Irwin killed a guy who tried to rob him on the LA freeway."

That was the first time I had locked my stateroom door since coming aboard. I didn't like the feeling. And later, the C/M's lunchtime story didn't help my fears. His subject was pirates, not the swash-buckling buccaneers who always got the princess in old movies, but modern marauders in blue jeans.

"There's a kind of 'pirate triangle' defined by the Malacca Straits to the southwest, the Philippines to the east and Hong

Kong up north. The Malacca Straits themselves — between Singapore and Indonesia — are especially dangerous. Rumor has it that authorities in Indonesia are being paid off by the pirates. Ironically, Singapore on the other side makes law and order a cornerstone of their culture.

"Modern-day pirates have traded their corsairs for long, canoe-like powerboats — which can travel at speeds over twenty knots. When they overtake a merchant ship, they make fast to it with grappling hooks. A small group of men, usually not more than four or five, scramble to the deck and hightail it to the Captain's cabin.

"This is usually in the dead of night. They know the passageways will be empty then, except when the watches change around midnight and four A.M. The Captain is startled awake, usually with a knife to his throat, forced to open the safe and tied up afterward. The pirates can make a clean quick getaway because the rest of the crew doesn't even know they've been boarded.

"Every merchant vessel carries cash aboard. An American ship might have $20,000 or $30,000: mostly for advances to the crew. So piracy, especially on *our* ships, can be quite lucrative."

According to the C/M, a Sea-Land containership left Singapore in 1989, bound for Hong Kong. Pirates sneaked aboard as the ship was navigating the Straits. The amount of cash they took was never publicized, but rumor had it close to $30,000.

After that incident, Sea-Land ordered all their Singapore-bound ships to stand "pirate watches": laying out fire hoses to be used against anyone trying to grapple the ship. Another anti-piracy plan — reducing the amount of cash in the safe — was met with alarm by most of the Sea-Land Masters. They feared the reaction of criminals who didn't get what they wanted.

Just recently *Endurance* fell prey to a different kind of pirate. She anchored overnight off Hong Kong, waiting for dock space. No one heard anything unusual during the night (the Mate on watch stayed up on the bridge, checking bearings, and a single AB was roaming around the deck). But in the morning several containers, stowed on deck at the for-wardmost hatches and loaded with electronics like TVs and stereos, were found broken open. The contents had been lowered over the side and spirited away by boat. Since the thieves were selective — a container of electronics can be worth $500,000 — speculation was the pirates had help from the inside.

Fortunately, the fellows who're after cash or electronics don't usually kill. Both the pirates (and the officials they have in their pockets) know enough not to provoke an international outrage that would result in a clampdown of their activities.

The robbers of *Endurance* were never caught. Some specu-lated they were soldiers of the mainland Chinese army. The Hong Kong harbor police now patrol the anchorage. And *Endurance* keeps her fire hoses ready, plus a string of 500-watt bulbs with reflectors to light up the sides of the ship.

There is one other breed of pirate: the ship-hijackers. En-tire ships can be commandeered, the crews either killed or put ashore, and the cargo sold off — sometimes on the Inter-net. The stolen vessels are often renamed and reflagged, again with the help of so-called authorities. Others are broken up for the thriving underground business of selling scrap metal to shipyards. This kind of piracy, however, would hardly be possible with *Endurance*, a ship nearly three football fields long.

LATER

Mid-afternoon. Endurance *has dropped anchor off Hong Kong in the same bay where she'd been pirated, but I can't imagine anyone sneaking up on us because it's a crowded neighborhood. Several other containerships wait, like us, for a berth. Fishermen troll from small sampans, as their forefathers did when Hong Kong was still the sweet-smelling "Fragrant Harbor." A black submarine slinks off into the mist. Break bulk ships cradle lighters alongside. Their cranes — like beaks of mother birds — disgorge cargo, most likely the raw materials that feed the maw of Hong Kong's insatiable manufacturing machine.*

Chinese junks putt-putt by, their toothy carvings scaring off evil spirits. Fiberglass hydrofoils whisk impatient gamblers to Macao. Double-decker ferries scoot back and forth between Kowloon on the mainland and Hong Kong Island, their wakes weaving spiderwebs across Victoria Harbor.

Slabs of skyscrapers stand behind these aquatic players. I can picture the busy workers within, punching buttons, processing orders, transferring funds, and directing the moves of all these vessels, passengers and payloads. Hong Kong Island's Mount Victoria towers over all, showing off her 1,805-foot summit. On the bridge-wing, Bob puts his arm around me and whispers, "Didn't I promise to show you the world? Tonight we'll be at the top of Victoria Peak; I doubt if there's a more dazzling view anywhere else on earth."

"But I thought we had to anchor overnight . . ."

"Sea-Land knows the crew would mutiny if they couldn't get ashore in

Hong Kong. So it hires launches to take us in. You'll have to play Cinderella, though. The last boat back leaves at midnight."

I'm so excited I can't eat dinner. It's torture to watch most of the crew jump into the early launches. Finally, Bob is off watch and we get ready to board the 2015 launch. I do a double-take at two turbaned Indians standing at either side of the gangway. Bob explains, "British tradition, you know: using Sikhs as guards. We used to get them after we pulled up to the dock, but since the pirate incident, they come out to the anchorage on the first boat."

Our "launch" is an old hooker, probably a converted fishing boat, with two wooden benches on either side of the cockpit and a tattered canopy overhead. Our "Captain," standing at a spoked wheel with his back to us, looks creakier than his vessel. He's a Chinese caricature with his wrinkles, long shirt, baggy ankle-length pants and black sandals. From an opening in the bulkhead, a carbon copy of the skipper pops out, holding a dented saucepan full of water. I get a nice "no-thank-you" smile ready for this offering, but he steps in front of the wheelhouse and hurls the water at the windshield. This human windshield-washer, like a mechanical figure on a cuckoo clock, pops in and out, sluicing the salt spray away from the skipper's vision until we arrive safely at the dock.

Though it's now around 9 P.M., it could be New Year's Eve on Times Square. The sidewalks can't contain all the people who spill into the street. They, and an army of double-decker buses, block me from ogling the store windows. My eyes are pulled upwards toward skyscrapers ending in a vanishing point: abstract angles of glass with steel girders; circular windows punched into concrete. In this free-wheeling, free-market city where many common rules and regulations (like levying import and export duties) are overlooked, the architects seem to thumb their noses, too — at physics. I can't imagine these precarious shapes surviving the summer typhoons, though they consistently do.

There's no waiting in line for the funicular to Victoria Peak; everyone with any sense, it seems, is shopping. The attendant locks us into the car with authority. I have a confession to make: I really hate these things. It's a nasty mix of feeling trapped and disjointed, as we track upwards at a heart-thumping 45° angle. I repeat like a mantra the phrase I saw posted below: PERFECT SAFETY RECORD. When I finally dare look down, it's as if from outer space. The lofty skyscrapers have been reduced to their lighted outlines: a tiara of jewels encircling the harbor. No wonder the Hong Kong magnates who make it to the economic summit want to live on this mountain summit, gazing down from their pantheon on six million subjects.

DECEMBER 21

Endurance heaved up her anchor at daybreak, shifting to her berth at Kwai Chung Terminal, the world's largest container facility. On the bridge, Captain Harvey announced, "Please listen, everyone. Hong Kong Harbor Patrol wants us to look for bodies in the water. A fishing boat's been rammed by a barge."

No bodies, but a nightmare of buoys and boats in Victoria Harbor where marine rush hour never ends. By the time we docked, the Chief Mate was in high stress again. The final straw: no portable phone had arrived on his desk. He'd been pleading for one to communicate with the Sea-Land dock office: a long block from the ship. "They expect me to rush through everything; on *their* schedule, of course, so they can shove another ship in here . . . and still run back and forth like a hamster. Forget it! After I finish my paperwork, we're outta here."

This is great news: I've worried about getting lost on an errand for my son: buying the latest version of "AutoCad": a computer program for designing buildings, boats and vehicles. Software, like everything else in Hong Kong, is supposed to be a bargain.

After a stop at the Seaman's Club to use the clean bathroom and for Bob to change money, we jog right around the corner to the MTR — the Mass Transit Railway. The lobby is a vast cavern. Fortunately, the maps and instructions are written in both Chinese and English. Bob walks me through the Hong Kong money system and watches over my shoulder as I feed the machine six coins for two fares to Sham Shui Po. The imprint of a crowned Queen Elizabeth shows her looking serene and decades younger.

We join a wave of people funneling through the turnstile. Like schools of fish, everyone channels between pairs of yellow lines marking where the train doors will open. No shoving, papers or butts on the pavement, graffiti, or dirt in any form. No voice raised above a whisper. The train slides along on silken tracks. A female voice announces each stop — first in squeaky Cantonese, then dropping an octave to upper-class British. At the fourth stop, Bob grabs my hand and pulls me through the crowd. Half a dozen exits branch off from the Sham Shui Po station; Bob comments, "Ours you won't forget: it's called 'Fuk Wa.'"

He continues, "I think this is a neighborhood where the population density is ten times that of Tokyo. I'll bet there's multi generations in a couple of rooms, raising chickens and running businesses." Every window flies flags of laundry, strung out on long bamboo poles. Looking up, I see more flapping shirts than sky. I also watch the bellies of one 747 after another screaming toward Hong Kong's airport a few miles away, the wheels appearing to snag the buildings' rooftops. An addictive amalgam of chicken, garlic and peanut oil hangs in the air like Cantonese fog.

In the "Golden Arcade," a plain gray building, each of the three floors holds maybe fifty "businesses" with stalls the size of a flea market's. For very advanced fleas. Computer books, in both English and Chinese, are piled on tables, sharing space with every CD-ROM that's ever been made or copied.

My son Jeff gets his AutoCad, on a two-disk set with two dozen other programs. And the "Believing Bookstore" has a fax number and takes VISA.

Smug that we're off the tourist route, I suggest we eat like the natives. By now, Fuk Wa Street has geared up for lunchtime by turning itself into an outdoor mall and "food court." At one of the makeshift kitchens on the sidewalk, citizens slurp bowls of soup du jour, or dig chopsticks into mounds of rice with today's specialty poured on top. Unlike Pusan's Market, there are even folding chairs. Nearby, piles of girls' dresses, sunglasses, men's shirts, handbags, and cotton bra and panty sets provide post-lunch street shopping.

I pull away from Bob and peer into the steaming pots, trying to see what simmers within. And then I spot — wrapped around a pole next to one of the cauldrons — a very large, very alive snake. Bob, who stands where I left him, waiting for my inevitable return, grins. "No snake soup today, Madame?"

DOWNTOWN KOWLOON

LATER

With Bob returned to work, I'm now on my own and back on the MTR. I count the number of subway stops on my fingers, following the diagram on the wall (I can easily see over everyone's head) and double-check the signs *every time we hit a station. Good thing I've been keeping track; when the bilingual voice announces my stop, "Tsim Sha Tsui" it's an unfathomable slur of T's and S's. The slab of bodies — me in the middle — pushes out en masse. It travels down the platform, up the escalator, along a corridor lined with jewelry stalls, film kiosks and bakeries (but no eating allowed and no public bathrooms in the subway). Finally, we arrive at the southern end of Kowloon. Specifically, Nathan Road — the Chinese Fifth Avenue.*

Even here, I can't break free. The human slab moves forward for a couple of blocks, then gets stuck at a traffic light. Though I feel somewhat safe (no one is after my backpack or taking note of the blonde who has joined the tribe), my claustrophobia is rising. I edge over to the right, preparing to exit.

I've made a list for this day in the city I've always dreamed about:

(1) Buy last minute Christmas presents;
(2) Take high tea at one of the world's most famous hotels, the Peninsula.
    Jess said she'd try to join me around three, if she didn't have to pull
    a piston;
(3) Cram in as much as my feet can tolerate.

The Chinese Arts and Crafts stores funnel merchandise from the People's Republic into Hong Kong. The branch on Nathan Road is crammed with five floors of porcelain (delicate vases, bowls and tea sets), silk (bolts, blouses, dragon-lady dresses, lace-trimmed lingerie), jade in colors I never knew existed (purple) . . . as well as leather bags, foot massagers (I already need one), calligraphy supplies. I work my way up from the basement, which is stacked with packages of rice and noodles, a hundred kinds of tea, fruit candies, dried roots the size of small trees. It's a lot of bounty for a country of impoverished workers. I wonder if they ever see any of it.

I depart an hour later with a white beaded evening bag for my daughter-in-law, seed pearl necklaces for Bob's two sisters, peachy chemises and Chanel-style scarves for my friends, and a turquoise teddy for me. I'm aware I'm sending a bunch of American dollars via VISA, over to Communist China. I ponder how Hong Kong will change when the People's Republic takes it over in 1997. Will the "Made in China" goods edge out Cartier and Kenzo?

At the Peninsula Hotel, I wait for Jess in the Lounge lobby, re-reading the part in Born to Shop that brought me here:

> A tai-tai is the wife of a very wealthy Chinese man (a tai-pan) who has nothing to do with herself except to shop, eat lunch, and shop some more. She rests up from all this by taking tea at the Peninsula Hotel. It's getting to be chic for tai-tais to work — but not too seriously. They usually end up in jewelry stores that their fathers happen to own. Tai-tais are absolutely the most gorgeous women you will ever see, on or off the movie screen, and they dress only in designer clothing.

I was too embarrassed to walk through the front door of the Peninsula myself, dressed in cotton turtleneck, jeans, and my new "Reeboks" with their glue trim. Definitely not "tai-tai." So I rummaged in my backpack for one of my new Chinese scarves, knotted it around my shoulders, then positioned it off-center just the way one was draped over a creamy blouse in Chanel's window.

The Peninsula's tea room is called the "Lounge Lobby" because it sits right there, separated from the check-in windows by a brass railing. I spot several tables of exquisitely attired and coifed Chinese women whose pale faces advertise good breeding, expert makeup and frequent facials. No sign of Jess, unless she's had a complete makeover.

The Peninsula is as close to the old Empire as I will ever come. (Hard to believe Queen Victoria was actually annoyed when Britannia acquired her "silly little rock.") A polished stairway sweeps up to the mezzanine, where a string quartet strokes out Mozart sotto voce, so as not to overstimulate.

White plaster columns, ablaze with gold angels, soar upward to a celestial ceiling. A bellman, with his shiny buttons and little round cap, pads between tables, holding an oval sign with the callee's name chalked on — no shrill voice to interrupt the gossip. Waiters, in crisp white including gloves, bustle about with silver teapots and the other components — scones, sandwiches and petite pastries — of high tea.

I'm thinking of commandeering one of the serving carts, when Jess finally walks in. She's wearing bleached jeans and a long-sleeved knit shirt, her version of high tea attire. Over strawberry layer cake and a hot fudge sundae, we agree that what we like best about Endurance is that she carries us to civilized places like this.

The scenery inside the Peninsula is glorious, but it can't match the vision across the street. Kowloon's waterfront faces the skyline of Hong Kong Island across Victoria Harbor. As the sky molts from blue to lavender to mauve, the skyscrapers' lights flicker on to form designs: a cluster of mahjong flowers, Chinese characters, shooting stars and a mega-carat diamond. I. M. Pei's Bank of China thrusts its crystal column above its competitors — one being the Hong Kong & Shanghai Bank Building, reported to be the most expensive in the world at a cost of multi-billions.

At midnight, we're still shopping. Not for miniaturized electronics or for diamonds, rubies or pearls, like the Nathan Street patrons. Instead, Jess drags me off the beaten track to the Temple Street Night Market. We push through tables of watches and alarm clocks, Mickey Mouse pins with flashing eyes, eelskin wallets and lipstick holders, exercise tights, cassette tapes of Chinese pop tunes, "motorcycle" jackets, jogging suits. Unisex silk vests with rearranged Picasso faces look like a million bucks but cost just $10. It's impossible to separate the genuine from the fake, the bargains from *the rip-offs. No matter. It's noisy, flashy; currency is flying and plastic bags are overflowing. This street fair for the locals is the kind of place where merchant mariners feel right at home.*

A final impression of Hong Kong's night market: the shellfish eaters. Undershirted men lounge over small tables set out on the roped-off street, greedily sucking steamed snails from their crazy-quilt shells. Like whale sharks, who must ingest tons of tiny krill to sustain life, the men eat rhythmically, throwing the casings to the ground as they wash the meal down with beer. Under their feet, discarded shells crunch to a white powder on this urban beach.

DECEMBER 22

Everyone has worked hard to ensure Endurance *will sail on time. The pre-sailing gear tests are complete, the whistle has sounded, the engine's all warmed up. The deck department has finished the stowaway search, including the emergency escape tunnels from the engine room. The two ABs replacing Clark the Budweiser Man and Irwin the Possessed caught their flights from the States, arrived on time, and have been signed on. All are present and accounted for — except the Radio Operator.*

Now I wonder if it was prophetic: Keith asking me, as he set off for downtown, "Could you make a sign to put around my neck, saying IF FOUND SLEEPING, PLEASE RETURN TO SEA-LAND EN-DURANCE BY 0700?" And Hong Kong is the one port that cuts you no slack. Endurance *is forced to leave the dock at her scheduled sailing time: 0800. One of Sea-Land's feeder ships has closed in; her smokestack appears raised and ready to fight for her space.*

The Captain has no choice but to anchor out, since ships can't legally sail without a radio operator. While he's pacing the bridge with the Hong Kong pilot aboard and two tugs standing by, he gets a call from the shoreside office: a taxi has just deposited Keith. They're sending him out in a launch.

The Captain tells the Chief Mate, "Go meet the sonofabitch down at the main deck, and don't lower the gangway. He's going to have to use the ladder."

Bob calls to me as he runs out of the office, "I've grabbed both our life preservers. If Sparks is as drunk as I think he is, I'll probably have to jump in after him."

I watch Keith anxiously, his extra weight a turtle's carapace as he struggles up the rope ladder hand-over-hand. Will he fall? Can he swim? Will I have to save him by diving into the "Fragrant Harbor?"

Chapter 20

THE EAST CHINA SEA

DECEMBER 23

Some sage has said that today's People's Republic of China is a cross between Dodge City and Dickens' London. Excited to hear that *Endurance* would be calling at Shanghai, the former economic capital and the most westernized of Chinese cities, I got the required yellow fever and cholera shots before leaving the U.S. I knew that after all the years of gray somnolence and decay under Communist rule, the once-worldly city was struggling back to its former glory, with stores displaying European fashions and serving up Kentucky Fried Chicken. Mao's dictum to "serve the people" has mutated into multimillionaire comrades serving foreign investors.

In 1979, two American ships called at Shanghai after a hiatus of 30 years. Others followed. Now Sea-Land wants to establish a presence. The Captain has received a pile of faxes from another Sea-Land Master. The latter was sent to check out Shanghai for the company, as it prepares to bring in large containerships. The Master notes that "It takes four cartons of cigarettes to grease your way through the authorities." The main problem is the Yangtze River's eight-meter depth. Because the ships will be heavier leaving than arriving (more cargo picked up than discharged), they must be turned around before docking. The turning basin — even shallower than the river — can be used just twice a day, at high tide.

The Captain and Chief Mate are poring over the navigational directions, studying the fuel weights and cargo distribution, and playing with different scenarios for ballasting. The cadet is frantically transposing Chinese meters to American feet, and back again. He's all too aware what will happen if he screws up.

Ballasting and deballasting of water are used for a ship's stability and to trim it fore and aft. *Endurance* has nine ballast tanks. When she encounters dirty water, such as in Shanghai, she can avoid taking on local ballast by shifting her own ballasting around from tank to tank.

When cargo loads change at different ports, ballasting or deballasting may be required. The International Maritime Organization (IMO) has a voluntary code that requires a vessel to "flush" tanks that have been ballasted in foreign waters. Each tank is emptied, then refilled with the clean water of the open ocean. This is to allow "alien" marine species, disastrous to indigenous marine organisms with no natural predators, to be discharged into the vast, neutral sea. Careless deballasting has caused zebra mussels to invade the Great Lakes, Japanese starfish to destroy Australian reefs and American comb jellyfish to float through the Black Sea. Pathogenic viruses, bacteria, and toxic marine algae can also be transferred via ballast water.

Now, as we inch upriver toward our Shanghai mooring, I think about the Yangtze in fact and fiction — from the Opium Wars to World War II. A symbol of the New China glides downriver — it's Cunard's Royal Viking Sun with a payload of international passengers.

The Chief Mate carefully checks the draft fore and aft. The Shanghai dockmaster now proclaims the ship must not draw more than 7.5 meters. We drop the anchor near the mouth of the Huangpu River, a tributary of the Yangtze ("Chiangjaing" on the chart). It's a raw, rainy day; the river is liquid mud and smoking factories blot out the skyline off to port. We can see the outline of a new city — Pudong — rising eerily behind the rain and smog.

Ever so slowly, with the help of two Chinese harbor pilots and two tugs, Endurance gets safely turned around, then docked at the Ching Kung Lu terminal. But the usual excitement of going ashore — even in a less than perfect place — is missing. Why? Because no one is getting off the ship! It seems that Sea-Land overlooked a United States-China reciprocal pact and neglected to provide visas. From the Captain down to the wiper, we've a discontented crew. We hear that Mr. Lai, the company's Hong Kong rep, is flying in to see what he can do.

Meanwhile, just in case, I'm scrutinizing a sheet of instructions that one of the Chinese pilots left on the chart table:

SOME IMPORTANT RULES/REGULATIONS
FOR ENTERING THE PEOPLES REPUBLIC OF CHINA

(1) ALL CREW MUST BE BACK BEFORE 0200 HR. ANY
    LATE-COME-BACK WILL BE FINED. ACCORDING
    TO THE LOCAL REGULATION NO. 89, NO CREW
    MEMBER CAN STAY ASHORE OVERNIGHT
    UNLESS APPLICATION SUBMITTED TO THE
    FRONTIER POLICE THROUGH THE AGENT IN

*ADVANCE AND APPROVAL OBTAINED. THE
HOTEL RECEIPT MUST BE PRODUCED TO THE
FRONTIER POLICE ON WATCH AT THE GANGWAY
WHEN THE CREW MEMBER COMES BACK.
(2) THERE ARE LOTS OF PEOPLE ON THE STREET
OFFERING MONEY CHANGE. IT IS ILLEGAL.
(3) IT IS VERY STRICT THAT NOBODY CAN HAVE
SEXUAL RELATIONSHIP WITH NO PROPER
MARRIAGE.*

A frontier policeman is stationed on the dock — young, unarmed, under-outfitted for the damp cold. He paces back and forth, unable to get warm and bored to death, I'm sure. I feel sorry for him and wave down; he waves back. I suspect this will be the sum total of my interaction with the locals.

What's surprising, given the drabness of this place, is the colorful cranes. Each crane's "legs" end in red-striped "feet," each having three toes. They could be Sesame Street critters if they weren't moving cargo. The stevedores are jabbering away in Chinese. The Chief Mate fervently hopes the containers will be loaded such that the ship's draft and stability will not be compromised — and Endurance won't get glued to the bottom of the Yangtze when she leaves.

Meanwhile, Mr. Lai has arrived aboard, complaining loudly about the inefficiencies of Shanghai's airport, road system and taxi drivers. He's just in time for a medical crisis. Joe, the tattooed AB, already skeleton-thin, has been experiencing severe vomiting and diarrhea. After repeated phone calls to someone called "The General," Mr. Lai receives permission to take Joe to the nearest hospital.

When Joe returned, he reported to the Chief Mate's office to drop off his "Request for Medical Treatment" form, which lists the doctor's diagnosis and treatment (antibiotics in this case). He looked even worse than before he went ashore, not surprising since he described the hospital as "something you'd expect in Sarajevo: dark and cold . . . only the doctors' section was heated . . . paint peeling, half the light bulbs out. The X-ray machine looked to be vintage 1920s. On the way back, we drove by a section of new apartment buildings, which the driver said was built to attract foreigners. It was nearly empty, with no lights on."

Yet, another AB we know who's been to Shanghai has reported that the city is bright, alive, full of women more beautifully made up and more stylishly dressed than in Hong Kong. The Bund, the famous waterfront area, has imposing European-style buildings and a lovely promenade; you can see a top-drawer nightclub show at the Peace Hotel for only $10, and buy a silk dress for $12. The AB maintained that he and his fellow seamen found Shanghai far more fascinating than Hong Kong and think it will be the new hot spot of the Far East.

On the basis of these contradictory first-hand accounts, I'm more determined than ever to see Shanghai. I make Bob promise to bring me back, and by some other means than a containership. "Can you imagine trying to get a sense of centuries of Chinese culture, in just twenty-four hours?" I ask with sound reasoning. Finally, I understand the frustration behind John McPhee's remark: join the Merchant Marine and glimpse *the world.*

The night turns into a nightmare. Coming off watch, the Captain accosts Bob, "Joe seems to be having an allergic reaction to the medicine they gave him at the hospital. You need to check his vitals." Bob goes down to the AB's room and finds Joe seized with muscle spasms. "The General" won't let the patient return to the hospital, but does summon a doctor to the ship. Bob falls into bed and is roused an hour later when the doctor arrives. Bob tells me she's young and gorgeous, with flawless skin. A nurse is with her, who interprets in English. They theorize Joe may be suffering from epilepsy.

As soon as Bob crawls back into bed, the phone rings again. "Third Mate here. The stevedores left a stacking frame unsecured, and it's just lying on top of another one." This was the first time Bob ever saw this happen. So the Chief Mate drags chain out of the Bosun's locker and he, the Bosun, and two ABs struggle to secure the frame for an hour and a half. Then up to the bridge for the 0400 watch.

DECEMBER 24

The exhausted Chief Mate faced one last problem when he went down his departure check list. A message from Mr. Lai warned,

"Now it is the time for the breeding of the baby fish. All the fishing boats grab the high tide to spread out all their nets to catch their 'gold,' the baby fish. The whole sea can be covered with nets and fishing boats tied up with each other, blocking sea traffic, even small craft like the pilotboat."

With care and a lot of praying, however, *Endurance* was able to reach the deep water of the East China Sea without running aground. In Shanghai, she loaded on containers full of stuffed toys ("cupid teddy plush"), machine screws, Christmas decorations, tires, jute luggage, multi green kitchen towels, acupuncture needles, water chestnuts sliced, chains, hooked rugs with latex, hand tools, and "dressed coat hair." Examining the manifest, I felt for the first time the collaboration ironies of today's international trade. Manufacturing jobs in the U.S. are in jeopardy as American companies turn to skilled workers and lower wages abroad. Chinese workers happily bring home pennies a day, turning out products for America which were once made there. And the U.S. shipping industry participates willingly in this international goods shuffle for the benefit of its own bottom line.

PART IV

"Where Sky and Water Meet"

And we were once again upon the ocean, where sky and water meet.

Richard Henry Dana

Chapter 21

FIVE HUNDRED MILES NORTHEAST OF SHANGHAI

DECEMBER 25

Christmas at sea. Like Thanksgiving, it's another poignant day for those of us with families. We don't even share the same holiday; theirs comes a day later, because of the International Dateline. Enroute to breakfast, we find that Santa must have used his electronic "GPS" to locate our small speck on the big ocean: tree ornaments dangle from every stateroom door. "JOY," spelled out in red sequins, dangles from ours.

Though work-wise this could be just any day, the baking smells from the galley, which began before breakfast, are a pleasant distraction. Today, I've willed myself to be hungry at 1130; a good thing, as Louis has gotten his act together. We heap our plates with shrimp cocktail and fried calamari; roast beef and turkey; candied yams and creamed onions; pumpkin and mincemeat pies; pound cake and ice cream; nuts. A bowl of wrinkled apples and oranges have saved their last breaths for the big event.

Smiling slyly, the Captain produces a bottle of Glen Ellen chardonnay; my one glass makes me so lightheaded, I take to my bed after the meal. Ghosts of Christmases past float around the stateroom while I toss restlessly, tangled in the sheets.

Later in the afternoon, Bob rings from the bridge: "Hurry up here . . . you'll see something really strange." Indeed! Off to starboard, what appears to be a trillion tufts of troll hair poke out of the sea. "Sea smoke," Bob explains. "It comes from the warm Kuroshio Current colliding with cold air. The water temperature's around 70° and I'll bet the air's no more than 40°. The last time I saw sea smoke was on the Alaska run."

"All kinds of crazy things happen out here. The Captain once told me about an incident when he was a Second Mate, standing a bridge watch. During a lightning storm, a huge ball of St. Elmo's fire shot into the wheelhouse, rolled along the deck, and flew out the opposite door. Neither he nor the AB on watch said a word to each other. Years later, they found themselves working together again and finally confessed they'd both seen the fireball.

"I've been in the same situation. A strange object once soared across the bow of my Navy ship. Again, no one on the bridge wanted to talk about it. I'm guessing that those of us who are scientifically trained go into denial when we see these weird phenomena."

As she did on the passage over, *Endurance* is taking the "great circle route" home — the shortest distance between two points on our planet's watery sphere. She'll head east for a few days to take advantage of the push from the Kuroshio Current. Then she'll trend northeast for the first leg of the great circle track. Everyone is talking about the Kuroshio Current like it's a big deal. I'd never heard of it before, so I open "Bowditch" — the mariner's bible:

> The Kuroshio (Japanese for 'Black Stream') is so named because of the dark color of its water. In

many respects it is similar to the Gulf Stream of the Atlantic. Like that current, it carries large quantities of warm tropical water to higher latitudes. The limits and volume of the Kuroshio are influenced by the monsoons, being augmented during the season of southwesterly winds, and diminished when the northeasterly winds are present.

Thanks to the current, bestowing knots like Christmas presents, we're making 26 over the bottom. The C/M is pleased: "We won't be able to keep this up once we're out of the current, but everyone's happy now — especially me, because I can *see* our speed on the knotmeter and know we're flying home. Even without the current, we'll be clicking off five hundred miles a day."

DECEMBER 26

It's been an unsettling couple of days. I feel disoriented: we're heading eastward from the Far East back to our west coast. The two new ABs are still adjusting to the daily routine and the new time zone they've flown into. One of them, Otis, has sailed on Endurance *before — as Bob's watchstander. Bob confided in me, "You can't help but like Otis: he's always so cheerful. There should be more African-American officers and Otis could easily pass the Third Mate's exam. The problem is he'd rather fall into a bottle than study."*

Rumor has it that the other AB, Eric, has done time in the Big House. The C/M checks a four-page "Deferred Employment Report" from Sea-Land listing the crewmen who have been suspended, put on probation or permanently deferred. Other seamen have made the list because of substandard performance, physical assault, breach of company policy or other offenses.

And then there is the continuing saga of Keith's Hong Kong adventure in his own words:

"That last night in Hong Kong, I set out to make the rounds. I remember starting out at the 'Kangaroo Pub' and trying to keep up with some Aussies. I lost. Then I went to 'Bottoms Up' where they shot some scenes for The Man With the Golden Gun. Someone dragged the cadet in. I'll never forget his face. I don't think Wisconsin has too many topless chicks in thongs, kneeling above you while they pour your drinks.

"Next I think, it was somewhere with a dance floor. I was having a grand time; thought I was John Travolta. I must have drunk two gallons of beer. But I did remember what time the ship was leaving and around 5 A.M., I caught a cab.

"Problem was: after I paid up and got out, I saw I'd been left on a dock all right, but it wasn't the right one. I wandered around for about an hour till I found another cab. There was still enough time to make the sailing. Then, can you believe it, we had an accident. It was just a fender-bender, but the police had to come. When we finally got back on the road, I was making such a fuss that I pissed off the driver who went extra-slow. I'll never forget running through the terminal and finding a feeder ship at our dock instead of Endurance.

"I guess the only reason the Captain didn't fire me on the spot was because he didn't have enough time to get another radio operator. But he rubbed my nose in what I'd cost the company — $17,000. That was overtime for the tugs, the pilots and the crew; plus the launch to bring me out. And he made it clear, 'If you ever pull another stunt like that, heaven help you!' "

Keith's Hong Kong adventure was only part of his story. His father, an overweight smoker, died of a heart attack when he was 53. He was also an alcoholic who had polished off a fifth of Scotch just before he died. When Keith discovered he was becoming just like his dad, he stopped drinking for five years.

Then six months ago, his second child was born with Down Syndrome. When the baby's circumcision was botched, requiring reconstructive surgery, Keith couldn't handle it and ran away to sea.

His wife feels abandoned and angry and he feels out of control. But missing *Endurance*'s sailing taught him that he has to get sober again. He promised he'd call AA as soon as we got to Long Beach. In the meantime, he wanted to work on his weight.

I told Keith, "I'm so sorry you've had all these problems, and I want you to know I'll help. The food part will be easy; the trick is never to 'diet.' Just watch how much the Captain puts away. But he doesn't eat meat, goes easy on sauces, and usually skips dessert. If you like, we can look at the menu together each morning.

"And how about jogging around the main deck with me? I have something to confess: I went down there in a storm once and almost got swept overboard. *I* could use a chaperone."

It was great to see Keith smile again. Someone was offering him constructive advice instead of criticism. And my nurturing nature had another hapless citizen to straighten out. In spite of the male myths, I was convinced that a woman on a working ship is not bad luck, but could be a force to offset depression.

DECEMBER 27

I awake to a rocking, frigid morning. As I pass by the radio shack, Keith calls out, "Welcome to Ice Station Zero." Glancing out his porthole, I could swear the waves are ridges of Arctic ice.

Forward, the containers lie beneath a snowy quilt. I grab Bob's hooded parka and tiptoe out on the bridge-wing into a universe of pure white, down drafts of snow mingling with spray. The ship is bucking as if trying to throw off the weather. This is no place for the faint of stomach, but something has changed since the passage out. I'm feeling more fascination than fear. Unconsciously, I've developed confidence in the ship, the warning radars, the engineers and navigators. Particularly the one I'm married to.

Instead of the weekly fire-and-boat drill, Ed the Engineer has arranged a field trip. He'll have Jim the First take us on a tour of the engine room. Could this mean a gold nugget lies inside Ed's facade of slate? He's saved us from the training film, which half the crew snoozes through and the other half snickers at. On hearing the news, Vince explodes. "Thank God! If I had to listen to that talking Switlik raft one more time, I'd have jumped overboard."

Before we start down, I ask Bob his impression of the engine compartment. He answers without skipping a beat: "It's a cross between Dante's Inferno and Frankenstein's lab."

Jess has already shared her thoughts with me, "The difference between the bridge and the engine room — especially in the summer months when warm water encases the hull — is like heaven and hell. Up there you're in air conditioning, looking at blue sky and clouds. Down below, it's searing heat, unbearable noise, oil and grease everywhere, and always the danger of fire."

I can't believe that despite Bob's story about the fire off Alaska, the fire-

and-boat drills and the safety films, I've never really thought seriously about a shipboard fire. All my anxieties have centered on external gremlins: storms, rogue waves, groundings, collisions.

The whole crew (except for the Captain, Third Mate and AB, who stay on the bridge and Ed the Chief Engineer, doing paperwork in his office) assembles on the main deck at 1015. The main deck holds the dock office, CO_2 room, air conditioner unit room, emergency generator room, paint room, incinerator room, soiled linen locker, fire alarm station, garbage room, dry provisions storeroom, dairy and vegetable room, freezer room with thaw box. (Amin once told me there used to be a dumbwaiter that helped him haul supplies up to the 01 deck, but the cable broke and some manager wouldn't ante up for another.)

Tucked into a corner of the main deck is a massive steel door with some serious rumbling behind it. If you aren't already intimidated, these five signs will do it:

CAUTION
High level noise area. Ear protection must be worn at all times.

NO ADMITTANCE

SAFETY
IS UP
TO
U

ATTENTION!
NO UNAUTHORIZED PERSONS ALLOWED

Warning:
This space is protected by a carbon dioxide
fire extinguishing system.

I'm both excited and nervous, as if I were about to witness open-heart surgery. The throbbing machinery has loomed large in my life since I joined the ship, but it's remained hidden and mysterious. Finally, it's my chance to be a dualie.

The door slams behind us as we follow the First down a flight of steep steel stairs. Immediately, unbelievable noise assaults us. Unlike the pulsating Ka-thunk Ka-thunk Ka-thunk *that permeates the upper decks, here it's a strident screech the Furies would understand. I appreciate the fashion accessories engineers always wear: a pair of earplugs on a string.*

Like Bob and Jess said, it's hot as Hades. Happily, Jim bangs a hard left into the control room at the base of the stairs. Here in an enclosed space the size of two end-to-end containers, the air vents discharge tolerable temperatures and the screech softens to the squeal of pigs being slaughtered. The control room is crammed with consoles, panel lights, circuit breakers, analog and digital meters, switches, computers with their printouts chirping away. This must be the Frankenstein part of the engine operation. Some of our group lean against the wall, but wouldn't it make Ed the Chief's day if my butt hit a significant switch? I scrunch down and seek the middle of the floor.

Jim begins his lesson, "The control room is never locked. That's because we don't worry about anyone stealing or sabotaging anything. Now let's talk about the fire alarms. We have smoke sensors in all critical parts of the ship: throughout the engine room of course, also in the cargo holds and paint lockers.

"Let's say you find a fire. There are four places where you can push a button for the fire pumps: on the bridge, in a compartment on the main deck, inside the shaft alley where the pumps live, and here in the control room. If the engine's been shut down, the buttons automatically fire up the emergency generator, delivering power to the pumps.

"We have about thirty hand-held fire extinguishers in the engine room. As far as I know, we've only had two bad accidents in the engine room. One time the fuel line cracked. Hot fuel oil — 400° centigrade — hit the inlet to the turbocharger. Another time . . . another crack . . . the engine room was black with tons of fuel. Fortunately, the fuel used for the main engine isn't the type that's likely to ignite.

"We store four emergency air packs — they're like SCUBA gear — in the engine room; the cylinder will give you fifteen minutes of oxygen." Bob, who's taken an advanced firefighting course, elbows me and whispers, "I don't think they'd last more than ten minutes, hardly enough time to rescue a buddy." Vince overhears and responds, "That's OK, I don't have any friends anyway."

The First Engineer passes out packages of foam ear plugs (visitors don't rate the professional model) and leads us into the Inferno. It is truly an underworld: a multi-level maze of massive pistons, compartments, stairs, ladders and tunnels. I can see Bob's point: if smoke fills up these spaces, how could you ever find — never mind rescue — anyone?

Dominating the engine room and towering over us, are the nine piston cylinders. Tubes snake out of their tops like a sea monster's tentacles. Three gigantic pipes, wrapped in insulating silver, connect with the main exhaust pipe suspended above. It's the size and shape of a grain silo. The main part of the engine lurks, like an iceberg, beneath a steel deck that surrounds the cylinders.

I feel like I'm back in school as we follow our leader single-file, past generators hefty as locomotive engines, and workshops that appear capable of rebuilding the entire ship. We pause to gaze down at the churning bronze propeller (Jim calls it "propulsion") shaft, two and a half feet in diameter.

I'm in awe of its power and apprehensive about a mis-step into the pit. Then Bob cracks me up with, "Ask them to show you the million hamsters they keep for emergency power."

Finally we come full circle to the exit door. I can relate to Orpheus ascending from Hades. How the engineers work in this noise and heat, day after day, I can't imagine. At least I have the satisfaction of knowing, as the sign above me proclaims:

YOU HAVE JUST SCALED MT. ENDURANCE

DECEMBER 28

After yesterday's monochrome snowscape, the muted colors outside my porthole seem extra-intense. The sea forms a gray-blue background for the ocean spray's brushstrokes of ivory. The clouds seen through the veil of Endurance's smokestack exhaust are smudges of ochre.

In the aftermath of the storm, ice is glued like epoxy to all the ship's surfaces. I dread Bob going out to read reefers since he won't let Ken risk it. I tell him so. The Chief Mate, who's been doing this all these years without a back-seat driver, curtly reminds me, "You forget, my dear, I'm a professional hatch-climber."

My worries are unfounded, because later I find Bob processing pre-Long Beach paperwork. Working on the unlicensed crew's overtime sheets, he complains, "Three ABs are 'over budget' (what Sea-Land allows them) so I'm going to thank them for their good work, then lay down the law: 'That's it for your overtime.' "

A sailor's overtime is the most sensitive issue on the ship. No seaman reacts in a neutral way to the subject of overtime —

especially *his* overtime. It can cause tension between un-licensed crew members and the ship's officers who lay out, grant, approve — and sometimes, disapprove — overtime. Or the source of stress can be between the vessel's manager, who typically represents the shoreside office, and the ship's officers in regard to *their* overtime.

Like workers ashore, a sailor's base wage, or salary, is based on a forty-hour work week, with normal hours between 8 A.M. and 5 P.M. But seamen don't knock off for the weekend at 5 P.M. on Friday. Ships must be manned, watched and worked twenty-four hours a day, 365 days a year, as long as they're transferring or transporting cargo.

So the crew goes on overtime, the largest share being that expended for weekend work. Aboard *Endurance*, the seven watch-standers (three Mates, three ABs, one Radio Operator) each put in sixteen hours every weekend. That's exactly one-third of the crew. Their overtime rate is based on the formula of 1.5 times their normal hourly rate — or "time and a half." Shipping companies have been fiddling with this sacred formula during the last few years in order to cap labor costs.

The Chief Mate's overtime rate is $36.56 an hour. He's third in the pecking order after the Master at $63.50 and the Chief Engineer at $57.76. Another reason why Chief Mates want to become Masters. There's little difference between the Second and Chief Mate's overtime rate: a mere $4.70.

Since overtime can amount to a large part of a seaman's wages, dayworkers have bargained for guaranteed minimums. The Bosun and his two deck workers, for example, generally perform maintenance work on deck. These non-watch-standers are guaranteed sixteen hours of overtime on weekends if they want it. They usually do. Also, the Steward's department is given weekend overtime, since meal preparation is a seven-day-a-week job.

I'm making a note of this for when I get back home.

DECEMBER 29

The crew of Endurance *must "lose" a total of nine hours over a twelve-day period — to catch up to California time. Each Captain uses his discretion on how to do this; Capt. Harvey tries to make it easy by posting clock changes for a couple of days in a row, then returning to a normal twenty-four-hour day, then repeating the pattern. I was fine for the first three nights but now when the bedside clock reads 0200, my body says "You can't fool me . . . it's only 2200."*

If I stay in my room, I'll sleep all day, which will foul up my circadian cycle even more. So I take my book down the corridor to the officers' lounge. It's the only place on the ship with a cozy feeling, especially at night when the overhead lights are off and the two table lamps are lit. There's dark paneling on two of the walls and a print of that stock Asian theme: misty mountain-with-waterfall.

The lounge is the size of a large living room; it's bisected by a beige steel room divider that houses the TV, VCR, and speakers. Facing the entertainment center are two lifejacket-orange couches, two swivel chairs in mustard vinyl, and a coffee table, covered with sexy magazines like "Marine Log," "Professional Mariner," and "American Shipper." There's a floor freezer stuffed with Breyer's ice cream and frozen yogurt, barbecued beef sandwiches, and mini-pizzas. An adjacent counter holds a microwave, popcorn popper, four-hole toaster, industrial coffee pot, and five-pound stainless canister which Amin keeps topped off with ground coffee.

An archaic refrigerator contains a sparse supply of fresh fruit, a plate of cold cuts and sliced American cheese, hard-boiled eggs, bread, butter, milk and mayo for "night lunch" — a shipboard tradition of snacks for the officers who stand night watches.

On the floor sit three garbage cans for PLASTICS, PAPER, GLASS & METAL. Coffee grounds are in the former, soda cans half-fill the "PAPER" container, and plastic cups and orange peels have been tossed in the "METAL" one. It makes one wonder how well the officers' licensing exams have weeded out the illiterate.

Ken the cadet is working with the Chief Mate on requisitions in the lounge. They are checking inventory against a master form; a list of supplies the ship will need for the next six months must be faxed to the home office.

He tosses the sixty-page form to me; one can order Lava soap, brooms, thirty different kinds of rope, ten sizes of batteries, clipboards, paint brushes and rollers, soldering guns, saw blades, back supports, ear plugs, flags, wrenches, inspection mirrors, air hoses, customs forms, freon, surgical gloves, funnels, stopwatches, tweezers, Polaroid film, hose clamps, ladders, rowlocks, smoke detectors. There is no order at all to this jumble. Still, for the C/M and Ken it's one-stop shopping: no running to Home Depot, then Walgreen's, then the supermarket.

In addition, it's imperative that the "ship's hospital" (two doors down from the galley — it figures) be fully supplied. Bob hands Ken a key and another thick list, telling him with a straight face, "Check it out. One of the things you'll see is a straightjacket, which we used on the last cadet." Because I peeked at this form too, I know Ken is also going to find "Amyl Nitrate Inhalants For Angina Pectoris" and "Bag, Mortuary Transfer, Leakproof Shroud Kit with Tags."

Theoretically, the officer tapped for medical duty can treat anaphylactic or insulin shock, asthma, bedsores, congestive heart failure, glaucoma, gonorrhea, gout, insomnia and stress, malaria, piles, poisoning, scabies and lice. On his last voyage, the C/M had to catheterize his Second Mate who couldn't urinate because of an enlarged prostate. The Emergency Medical Technician training the officers' union provides doesn't include delivering babies. It was always thus. When a bygone sea captain's wife accompanied her husband on the "hen frigate," as a sailing ship with a woman aboard was called, she was usually put ashore to give birth, then picked up many months later.

After too many hours of struggling with my laptop, I've swum from the murky purgatory of DOS into the bright light of WINDOWS. Here — with a click or two — I can cut & paste, add and subtract letters and words, even underline and be **bold** if I want to. Graduating from kindergarten to the first grade, the next step has to be PRINTING.

But there's a little glitch, which I share with Jess today at lunch. "You know, this huge printer sits right next to me on the shelf, but what if I screwed up CARGOMAX, the crew list, or the requisition program trying to hook it up? I'd probably be keelhauled."

"Worry not, kiddo," Jess replies. "You're welcome to use my printer."

Before I turn into the corridor past the workout room, I hear Beethoven's Ninth blasting from Jess' room. It's cranked up, I suppose, to drown out Willie Nelson who's serenading the Chief. "Are you surprised?" she asks. "Well, try this on. I started out as a music major. But I changed careers when I found out how hard it was to get a chair in a symphony orchestra." So Jess, like a butterfly mutating backward, changed her long black skirt into denim coveralls.

"I made another switch: from sailing to flying. My ex-husband and I lived aboard a gorgeous Hans Christian sailboat, but it cost so much to keep up, I let him have it in the divorce. After I got my airplane license, I wanted to be in the air all the time. One day, it was blowing like hell, but I took off anyway. I'd never done a crosswind landing; the Cessna got blown off the runway and flipped nose down. I wasn't hurt but the plane was totaled. I took the insurance money and went out and bought another one. Now I'm into aerobatics. For an adrenaline rush, you can't beat spins.

"Here's a picture of my Super Cub; I showed it to Keith who thought it was 'cute.' 'Wrong!' I told him; the word is 'macho.' And this is my boyfriend, Jamie, with his plane. Jamie works for American President Lines as a 'reefer'; that word can also mean a 'reefer mechanic.'"

Jess expertly attaches her printer to my computer, quickly configures it, and then hands me the first page of my journal in neat Times New Roman. It seems fitting that the technical expert and the technically challenged can share this moment of triumph. And I promise myself that I won't blow Jess's cover: like an M&M, her brittle exterior is soft and sweet inside, the Atalanta on our Argo.

DECEMBER 29

INTERNATIONAL DATELINE — ABOUT HALFWAY ACROSS THE PACIFIC

Here's that damn day back again. If I really were able to tamper with time, I'd push that magic button on the bridge and give us at least one of those twenty-five-hour days we had westward.

My old dark cloud has returned, the one that used to hang over me during a decade of Rhode Island winters. Too short days; too few rays. Then, I substituted martinis for sunlight; not too smart when I look back on it. I know sunny California will be popping over the horizon in less than a week. "So get moving, Girl," I tell myself and continue my exploration of the bridge.

At the rear of the bridge, activity centers around a twelve-foot long chart table. The current nautical chart is spread out on top, its corners held down by paper weights that resemble hockey pucks. (The other charts for this voyage are stored in the dozen drawers below.) The Mate on watch can look up from the chart and check a recording barograph, an automatic direction finder, a GPS and a "Sat Nav," a Dell computer (used principally for downloading weather data) and a Navtex receiver. The latter is used for receiving important Notices to Mariners, such as ships in distress, weather alerts and buoys out of position; it also prints out an hourly fix (in case the Mate forgets to get it off the GPS).

One would imagine a containership's bridge awash in computers. Sea-Land's main rival, American President Lines (APL), puts computers on *its* bridges. But Sea-Land's theory is this: if the watch-standers are fixated on their computers, they're not looking out to sea or into the radars. As a case in point, I've seen one Mate in particular, eyes glassy with fatigue, hypnotized by his screen-saver, which shoots out dots of colored "fireworks."

The bridge is also a maze of detectors, switches, fans, and buttons for either sounding a fire alarm or controlling a fire. As well as the usual fire hazards found on all ships, containerships have the added attraction of carrying flammable and explosive materials known collectively as HAZMAT. There are nine classes of Hazardous Materials:

- Explosives
- Gases — Compressed, Liquefied or Dissolved Under Pressure
- Flammable Liquids
- Flammable Solids
- Oxidizing Substances and Organic Peroxides
- Poisonous and Infectious Substances
- Radioactive Materials
- Corrosives
- Miscellaneous Dangerous Substances & Articles

In Hong Kong alone, *Endurance* loaded on calcium ("dangerous when wet"); hay ("flammable solid"); aerosol dispensers ("misc. dangerous substance"); toluene disocyanate ("poison"); ammonium hydroxide ("marine pollutant"); oxalic acid ("corrosive material"); ethylene oxide ("poison gas"). Happily, the HAZMAT manifest has a contact name/number to call if something blows up.

DECEMBER 30

It's Friday. How do I know that, with all the days running together and no sign of a weekend? Well, the menu is heavy on fish: shrimp omelettes for breakfast (the undersized shrimp sporting black "veins" and a tinny taste), broiled snapper at lunchtime and fried grouper for dinner. These fish were not flash-frozen in Alaska. The snapper hasn't snapped at anything for a while (indeed, I suspect it was pried from the side of Endurance's freezer), but the grouper fares better, disguised by heavy breading and frying oil. Overcompensating for the lack of flavor, I stuff myself. Now I'm sluggish and idle as a Queen Bee with twenty-two workers buzzing around me.

A new sheet of paper has been taped to the wall of the officers' lounge. It's an "Inter-Office Correspondence" from "Newt M." — one of Sea-Land's Vice Presidents. It reads:

SEA-LAND POLICY ON THE
SELECTION OF MASTERS

There has been some confusion about how Sea-Land selects its masters, which I have been asked to clarify. Some time ago, in order to eliminate possible personal biases in our selection of masters, we formed a Quality team headed by Alan and myself. We looked at our very best masters and compared them with our biggest screw-ups. We rated all of these masters on twenty-three variables, then had our Quality number-guru run a test on all this data — called "analysis of variance." (Believe me, this test doesn't lie!) We discovered that our very best masters are (1) young (2) Kings Point graduates (3) handsome. Our guru informed us that these three factors accounted for 89.9 percent of the variance between our "good" and "bad" masters.

Those of you who thought that "loyalty," "sea experience," and "company seniority," were important . . . forget it. Taken together, those accounted for only 4.6 percent of the variance. Why, even "breaks-wind-at-vessel-meetings" alone came in better than that — at 6.4 percent. So, to you guys who have been waiting around but don't meet the criteria, to you folks who spend twelve hours a day taking reefer temperatures, year after year (or doing whatever it is you do) . . . to you I can only say: YOU'RE GETTING PAID, AREN'T YOU?

As for those of you who are now sailing as master but who are also ugly (and you know who you are — we already identified eighteen on the permanent masters list), rest assured that we do not intend to interfere with your present assignment. Our official company policy is that just because you're ugly, it doesn't mean you're a bad person. Hey, look at your Uncle Newt — I'm not exactly Robert Redford myself!

When you're in town, drop by! And think QUALITY!

The notice has just enough plausibility to make everyone do a double-take. But soon the rumors start flying: who wrote it, masquerading as the V.P.? I'm not sure myself but I have heard the Chief Mate's typewriter working overtime lately.

"Well . . . yes," he confesses when I confront him. "But I'll deny it to my last breath. I've been obsessing a lot that I haven't been promoted to Master. I've never quibbled with Sea-Land about assignments — went wherever they sent me. Started out on a World War II tanker converted to a containership, on the Caribbean run. Then, I was assigned to two other relics, both times converted 'C-4's,' also left over from the war. In the early 1980s, Sea-Land had many vintage ships, which were dispatched one by one to a ship-scrapping yard after the company replaced them. After two years of tropical weather, I got the shock of my life when I was assigned to the Alaska run. Now fifteen years later, I'm still freezing my ass while the ring-knockers from Kings Point take care of their own."

I also puzzle over why Sea-Land has not taken advantage of Bob's abilities. He's super-smart, writes like the English major he was, can fix anything and knows all about the sea. He was well trained at Fort Schuyler to be a team player and bow to a Captain's authority. It bothers me to think that the Merchant Marine is not above playing the game of "it's-who-you-know."

Keith has been dropping pounds and getting compliments. And he's back to playing the good humor man. At lunch, he has Jess and me in stitches with tales of Boots, the farting cat, who fills his farmhouse with the smell of burning rubber bands. He also offers to show me around the radio room — aka "The Shack."

The radio room shares the 07 level with the bridge and is the size of a large walk-in closet. "We radio people work by ourselves, away from the rest of the crew," Keith says. "This fact seems to attract the weirdos of the electronics world. Two of my cohorts have had sex-change operations, and another was so paranoid he locked himself in and made everyone with a message shove it under his door.

"The RO's working schedule is one of the most normal on the ship. Basically it's keeping a radio watch from 0800 to 1100; 1300 to 1600; and 1800 to 2000. I get two hours off for lunch and dinner. When I'm off duty, I set an alarm for emergencies which rings on the bridge and in my room.

"Every morning, I notify Sea-Land of the ship's position via a marine telex called "INMARSAT A." Also, I send position reports to "AMVER" (Automated Mutual-Assistance Vessel Rescue) every forty-eight hours — so they'll know who's available to steam over if there's a distress call. In Japanese waters, they fine us if I don't report in every twenty-four hours."

The radio operator's most important duty is to monitor the 500 kilohertz band during the "silent period" of three minutes after the quarter hour and three minutes after the three-quarter hour. This is when all communication on this frequency ceases, except for distress signals. They still come in via Morse code, which we call "CW." Only five years ago, Sea-Land was still using CW instead of satellite systems as the principal means of communication.

The RO also sends out weather observations to the various Meteorological Centers and gets a weatherfax back twice a day, more often if there's bad weather. The printouts, which report on most of an entire ocean, go to the bridge so the ship can steer around severe storms.

In 1998 or 1999, a new distress and safety system will be required on all ships at sea. It will be about the size of a TV, whereas the current radio telegraph equipment takes up an entire wall. The RO worries his job will become obsolete, so he's thinking of starting an electronics repair business.

"In the meantime," Keith concludes, "There always seems to be a job for me on a ship. There are two unions for radio operators; mine has 220 members and I was the last person they accepted. When I joined in 1992, the initiation fee was $4,500; now it's $10,500. It wasn't a love of the sea that brought me out here; instead, I went down a list of electronics technicians jobs. This paid the best."

So even Keith, with his relatively easy job, has shipped out for the money rather than the adventure. It leads me to ponder how I would feel if I were another working stiff instead of the Supernumerary. From my perspective, this voyage is an adventure: new faces, places, and a way of seeing the world you can't order up through a travel agency. But for many seamen, the ship is their second home and their jobs aboard just as boring and repetitive as those in a factory. And they pay for their good salaries by constant work with few breaks. As the cynic Samuel Johnson said, "A ship is worse than a gaol. There is, in a gaol, better air, better company, better conveniency of every kind; and a ship has the additional disadvantage of being in danger. When men come to like a sea-life, they are not fit to live on land."

DECEMBER 31

Since we left the Kuroshio Current, Endurance has had this quadrant of the globe all to herself. Now suddenly, a target shows up on the radar. It's zipping along at 19 knots, directly into our path. The Chief Mate has Vince veer off 5° to starboard and twenty minutes later a freighter ghosts by, maybe a mile to port, the first ship we've seen on our long voyage home.

Yesterday's overripe bananas have disappeared from the breakfast bar. That was the last of them. The grapefruit, however, has ripened to sweet perfection. Bob says the old steward "Cinderella" would have mashed up the bananas in muffins, cake or his famous cream pie. But Louis is too busy watching videos. The milk has gone from fresh to frozen to a sterilized type in a cardboard box. "We call this Paul Hall Milk," Bob tells me. "Paul used to be president of the seaman's union and made sure his boys got their daily Vitamin D."

Louis has come to the ship's Medical Officer with a problem. Later, during his watch, Bob tries to describe it delicately: "He hasn't defecated for five days." Vince chimes in, "I can't understand why, with his excellent diet of sugar and flour." The two of them indulge in scatological banter; Vince comes up with various "remedies" — most of them involving the fire hose. Bob admits, "It's pretty bad when we're amused at someone else's expense. Guess we're constipated too — mentally and morally." Then turning serious, he says he's reluctant to add anything else to Louis' medicinal cocktails. The Steward has been medicating a bad back with codeine, penicillin, and some Chinese powders he picked up in Hong Kong.

JANUARY 1, 1995

We celebrated New Year's Eve last night by watching two of Jim the First's videotapes on fractals — psychedelic waves and mountains and crystals generated by mathematical formulas. The kaleidoscopic images, more spectacular than fireworks, shimmered to the music of "The Moody Blues." And all the while the ship felt like it was a wild thing, flying across the sea.

The weather has undergone a sea change, literally. The sun has come out from hibernation, the temperature has shot into the sixties and the water has turned a deep cobalt blue. Even the whitecaps look dolphin-friendly. It's the kind of weather that Bob and Ken have been waiting for, to go out and count twistlocks.

Twistlocks are fist-sized metal castings, weighing approximately ten pounds, which fit into the corner castings of containers and lock them together vertically. Several years ago a new feature emerged: a self-locking model. Spring-loaded jaws clamp the corners together when one container drops atop another. This means that longshoreman no longer have to put themselves at risk by clambering around upper tiers to lock them manually.

Because twistlocks are such a critical item, Sea-Land requires an inventory to be taken every voyage home; 1370 is the magic number that must be aboard. The Far Eastern longshoremen have dropped the extras in bins and the C/M must lay them out on deck, count them, then put them back in. The C/M has calculated that he moves five and a half tons of twistlocks around in the space of two hours. He used to have the Bosun do this job, but once he came up one hundred short. When the C/M ordered this number to make up the loss, he received a blast from the vessel manager. And then he discovered the Bosun's count was wrong, a further embarrassment. Since that time, the Chief Mate has done the counting — and lifting — himself.

JANUARY 2

Yesterday, while jogging around the 06 deck with Keith, three fat petrels soared around us, riding the ship's thermals. Why was this ménage à trois two thousand miles from land, I wondered. Where were they migrating to? They seemed utterly confident and carefree. I thought of all the sophisticated navigational equipment on Endurance, *compared to the birds' minuscule control centers. And we humans refer pejoratively to "birdbrains."*

Today, I'm on the main deck, waiting for Keith. As I do a warm-up lap, I find one of the petrels lying on his back, wings tucked in and head resting on one shoulder, yellow legs and feet stretched out. At first I think he's sleeping but he hasn't moved when I come around again. I don't want to face the fact that he's dead.

I climb back up to the bridge in tears, the first I've shed on the ship. I feel real grief and ask, "Can I talk it out with Dr. Bob?" He thinks I'm over-reacting but indulges me, anyway. "Well, I suppose it's the frailty-of-life thing: the swift random way you can lose it. Yet, these creatures who fly out into the ocean are so adventurous, brave, and far from home. I think you see some of yourself in them . . . coping with danger on a daily basis makes you feel both fragile and special."

Vince interrupts, "I've got the answer, Mate. We could have a little ceremony: bury the bird at sea and put in for extra overtime." Irony and the tough-love approach bring me back to reality. Sure enough, a dogged-down page of Two Years Before the Mast reveals that "An overstrained sense of manliness is the characteristic of seafaring men. This often gives the appearance of want of feeling, and even of cruelty. . . . A 'thin-skinned' man could hardly live on shipboard. One would be torn raw unless he had the hide of an ox. A moment of natural feeling for home and friends, and then the rigid routine of sea life returns."

If men are historically unwilling to show their emotions, it's no wonder these abnormally long stints together lock them in an emotional freezer. I, on the other hand, without the distractions of friends and chores, find all my senses sharpened. Over-emotionally, I made the petrel symbolize my own life's losses. The little bird, however, almost made it across the big ocean, and undoubtedly had fine adventures along the way.

JANUARY 3

The time changes have brought us late sunrises: around 0930. My body rebels against crawling out of the covers in pitch blackness (Sea-Land *certainly wouldn't want me on the 4 to 8 watch.) But there was one small reward this morning: I saw Jupiter snuggling up against the snippet of a new moon.*

Today I'll be attending the ship's first safety meeting. The C/M tells me on the way down to the crew lounge, "Until recently, the officers merely paid lip service to safety meetings. Now the company insists that the whole crew attend. It's a good idea, since there's no way we alone could uncover all the problems. Accidents are a shipowner's third highest expense after fuel and labor."

The Captain first compliments the C/M. He reads a bit from the Sea-Land's newsletter "Insight":

> *Safety practices often result from practical experiences. Chief Mate Robert Allen, of the M/V Sea-Land Endurance, working with his Boatswain, devised a system to secure the gangway stanchions by means of rope straps. These preventers have significantly reduced the movement of the stanchions, eliminating the risk of future injury.*

I am very proud of my Chief Mate's ingenuity but later he gives me the behind-the-scenes dope. "The stanchions are hinged, and lowered when not in use. But if a seaman working around the gangway is stupid enough to grab one of the lowered stanchions for support, it can pop right out. We had two injuries in quick succession — one causing an AB to lose all his front teeth. The Sea-Land safety manager fired off a fax asking what was going on. So I worked up a simple little solution and informed Sea-Land the problem had been taken care of. They sent me a watch and Endurance got $1,000 to spend on safety equipment. I plan on ordering the crew asbestos jock straps."

At the safety meeting, I picked up a *Sea-Land* bulletin called "Safe Ships / Clean Seas." It featured an interesting story about an incident on another ship:

"One day prior to arrival in Tokyo, the Bosun was working in the area of the port gangway when he fell outboard over the side of the vessel while it was underway at full sea speed. He was no stranger to this vessel, having been Bosun aboard her for the first ten years of her life. While it is not totally clear if the Bosun hit his head and blacked out or if he passed out while working, the next thing he remembers was dangling at the end of his safety line, his whole weight suspended by the belt and spanner wire. He called for help and was pulled to the deck by four crew members."

The tale had a happy ending: although the Bosun broke a rib, he did *not* fall overboard and get sucked into the ship's propeller. And Sea-Land has a new rule: everyone in the cargo loading area must wear a hard hat. Several years ago, a worker was killed by a container while lubricating a stacking frame on the dock. Can a hard hat really protect workers from flying containers?

JANUARY 4

Today's goal was to drag a blanket up to the 06 deck and pour peroxide on my hair. It's grown a pale green streak down the back (probably from standing too long under the shower), which has been drawing some curious stares. Instead, I find that California has announced its proximity with a fog bank. Someone has just whitewashed the world, covering all its hues with a chalky sponge, turning the sun to a pale silver. I squint my eyes, but there's nothing to focus on, which gives me vertigo. Suddenly, as if I'd willed it, a fuzzy horizon pierces the mist and restores my equilibrium. The sun returns to a polished bowl dripping a strip of mercury onto the water.

My father — who died fifteen years ago — comes back to me. He'd been a weekend watercolorist; I loved to watch him soak a sheet of thick d'Arches paper in the bathtub, then use a #10 brush to lay on Payne's gray washes. When he tilted the paper back and forth, up and down, the washes made hazy clouds. Above me is that same watercolor sky, and I can feel my father as close as if I were standing next to him. I huddle in front of the engine's vent, letting it warm my back. Now comes a jagged break in the clouds . . . sheets of sunlight cascade from it like a waterfall. A transcendental outpouring, then the clouds bleed back together. Though the temperature is in the upper sixties, I begin to shiver.

An infectious disease is running through the ship. Called "channel fever," it's the excitement sailors feel when approaching land after a long sea passage. The sailors on the brig Pilgrim spent those last days at sea "putting the ship in the neatest order. No merchant vessel looks better than an Indianman, or a Cape Horner, after a long voyage, and captains and mates stake their reputation for seamanship upon the appearance of their ships when they haul into the dock."

Instead of bringing the ship back to Bristol fashion, Endurance's crew obsesses about ending their deprivations, and the desire seems more for food than loved ones. Keith relives the searing Indian curry he had in Hong Kong. Jess walks us through every step of her bananas sautéed in Cointreau. I try to create a mouth picture of my favorite Greek salad: orzo, hunks of feta cheese, Calamata olives and fresh basil, all marinated in extra virgin olive oil and lemon juice. All these succulent goodies await us just over the horizon — we hope.

The last night at sea, three wonderful events take place:

(1) The coast of California shows up clearly, with all its bumps and indentations, on the weatherfax map.

(2) The Armed Forces radio and its interminable ball games are replaced by a dozen shoreside stations on the radio's broadcast bands.

(3) Louis, afraid of being fired perhaps, puts together a cookout. He sets up a grill on the deck. We take our plates outside for Louis to load on the chicken, steak or sausage (for many of us it's all three), then fill in the empty spots with corn, baked beans and garlic bread. Our "backyard" is a silvery sea rushing by, but still the crew grouses: "What's a barbecue without beer?"

PART V

"It's Time For Us To Leave Her"

Oh, the times are hard and the wages low,
Leave her, Johnny, leave her;
I'll pack my bags and go below;
It's time for us to leave her.

Old Sea Chantey

Chapter 22

BACK IN THE U.S.A.

JANUARY 5

As a welcome-home gift, the Port of Long Beach presents us with a postcard day. Mid-70s, blue sky spotted with cottony clouds, diamond facets scattered across the sea. Outside the harbor, dozens of sailboats have come out to play, darting around Endurance's *hull. I wave down, the sailors wave back. My perspective has definitely changed from my old boating days: I am the superior high up on this black hull.*

Oddly, the M/V Endurance *is the only containership pointed toward the port. One of the shipping magazines in the lounge had me convinced we'd be only one fish in a big school of commercial vessels:*

> *The Port of Long Beach is the busiest containerport in the U.S., with over 2,000 containerships calling in 1994. Upcoming years will bring greater cargo volume, as transPacific shipping companies bring into their fleets new, larger containerships capable of hauling 5,000 TEUs (a 25% larger carrying capacity than current ones possess).*

Keith pops out of the radio room to join me on the bridge-wing. "Some sight, huh?" he says, pointing to starboard. "Those landmarks signal 'This Way to Long Beach'." The three poppy-red and black smokestacks of the Queen Mary are distinctive navigational aids. I watch the luxury liner, launched in 1936 and once the undisputed queen of the sea, come closer. I think of her heroism during World War II, when she ferried divisions of U.S. soldiers to Europe. She was able to evade all of Hitler's U-boats, with a $250,000 price on her head, only to become a Long Beach tourist attraction.

I've heard that it took eight tugboats to maneuver the Queen Mary — 159 feet longer than we are — into port. And here are two tugs twirling our ship around in a turning basin, then backing her into the dock as if she were floating on a cushion of air.

Even before Endurance's mooring lines tighten around the bollards, several cars approach with determination down the dock. Significant others emerge, some with small children in tow, and search aloft. All they find is my face as everyone else is still working, and I receive some uncertain stares. I feel I should shout down, "Don't worry . . . I'm legal."

Standing out from a fleet of Sea-Land trucks, two well-polished CUSTOMS and IMMIGRATION cars glide up to the gangway. The Chief Mate had warned me, "Have your passport and customs declaration ready. Please don't embarrass me by disappearing into the workout room. Everyone has to be checked off before the ship is cleared."

So I'm sitting dutifully at my desk, waiting to be called, when Bob storms in. "I can't believe the bastard; I wonder where his brains live, assuming he has any," he sputters. "Louis. Just walked off, said he was looking for a phone to rent a car, then sauntered back. The Immigration folks are furious; they're threatening to retaliate and hold up the whole ship."

"Well I don't know why you're surprised," I answer. "Louis is a video vampire: he's devoured every film on the ship and is desperate for a fresh fix." The Chief Mate does not think the Supernumerary is either amusing or in order.

While Bob and the crew placated the powers that be, I observed something called "bunkering." I'd heard rumors we were going to do this in Long Beach and asked Jim the First what it meant. He answered, "It's what recreational boaters call refueling. *Endurance* can fill her tanks in California and carry enough bunkers — fuel — for the entire voyage. Or she can shop the Far East market and bunker with cheaper fuel over there. This voyage, we bunkered at the beginning and ran so low, we came in on sludge this morning. Had to rev down to 95 rpms.

"Now if we do use foreign fuel, we try to get it tested up front. Bad fuel not only stops you dead in the water but can ruin engine parts. We try to keep bunkers from different ports separate because mixed fuel often waxes up.

"When the fuel barge pulls alongside, she'll disgorge 3200 tons of heavy fuel oil into *Endurance's* tanks. The ship's diesel engine burns about ninety tons of this stuff on a good day, more when the seas are rough, the currents strong, the bottom dirty, and the cargo or ballast heavy."

The two-hundred-foot barge tied up alongside. A small crane rigged on *Endurance's* 02 deck hauled up a long reinforced neoprene hose. A flange at the end of the hose was mated with its partner on the ship's fuel manifold with half a dozen bolts. With the flanges held securely in place, the fuel flowed from barge to ship. The whole procedure could take up to twelve hours, depending on the temperature of the fuel. Pity the poor engineers stuck in the engine room, staring at the gauges and directing the fuel flow into eight pairs of port and starboard tanks.

At lunch, everyone at the table seems all steamed up. Bob declares, "It's not been the greatest morning of my life. I had the whole deck department practically standing at attention for the Coast Guard inspection, and they were an hour late. That screwed up discharging the crew and signing the new ones on. Then one of the fire hoses sprang a leak. That got written up. But here's the last straw. The 'Medical Officer' on the last voyage was supposed to check the dates on all our meds; he forgot. So the Coast Guard found that we've got a bunch of expired drugs and won't let us sail until we replace 'em."

Jim chimes in with his own gripe: "One of the suppliers charged a $100 drop-off fee for delivering less than four drums of lube oil. And Sea-Land spends around $350,000 a year on this ship's lube oil alone."

In the afternoon, the Chief Mate's office is bustling with new crewmembers waiting to sign on. Long Beach, being the "designated payoff" port, means that most of the crew changes over here instead of in Oakland. At payoff, the crewmember can choose to get his money by check or in cash. The more trusting choose cash, and I wonder how much of it leaving the ship today will be in someone else's pocket tomorrow.

At least one of the departing crew members has the tax man snapping at his heels. The story goes that he was known as a real player around the union hall, willing to bet on anything. He was also impressionable. He once sailed with a Radio Operator who belonged to a national anti-

taxation group. The crewman wasn't politically inclined, but he clearly saw that his tax funds might be put to better use at the race track. Now the day of reckoning has come.

Keith pushes through the crowd to hug me good-bye. "You be good now, y'hear?," I whisper.

"I promise," he replies. "I mean, I really promise. I've already arranged to go to an AA meeting tonight."

Since Keith has started to take care of his body, I hope that putting his head right will be the next step, since he is one of the few crew members for whom life ashore is more stressful than at sea. And with the radio officers on ships still in demand, it will be all too easy for him to "run away to sea" again.

It's sad to lose some of my new-found friends. I want to take Amin home with me; without him our bed will never be made with such military precision. At least I won't have to interact with Ed any more, and he remains sullen to the end. Dr. Bob, clinical psychologist, diagnoses Ed's problem: "He's never married his long-term live-in, so she can't join him. Therefore, he feels no other couple — like us — should be together on a working ship."

A new cast of characters begins to fill the stage. Jake, a Filipino cook, replaces Big John. He makes a little bow when we're introduced and says, "I'm sorry you'll be leaving us, Miz Allen. But I hope you'll have dinner on board tonight; I'm making something special."

The one I was really waiting for was a woman. Jess had told me that Rusty (the Third Assistant Engineer) would not be making a back-to-back voyage. So she wrote a twenty-year buddy, Denise, that the position might be available. Jess, ordinarily a cool cat, did verbal handstands when she heard that her chum's shipping card was old enough to snag the job. On *Endurance's* upcoming trip, there would be two female officers in the engine room.

When Denise shows up in the office to sign on, I'm surprised. I expect her to be a carbon copy of Jess, as the two of them have been together in marine engineering since the late 1970's, when female officers joined the American Merchant Marine. But Denise is as rounded as Jess is taut. She even has breasts. Denise looks more like a teacher than an engineer, with wide eyes behind thick rimless glasses. Protruding teeth in a malleable mouth, turned up at the corners, give her a quizzical expression, as if she is pondering a droll joke. She reminds me of someone . . . Yes! Diane Keaton.

And I actually see a different Jess later: relaxed, with her body slack in her chair and her feet propped up next to her computer. "Well, Dennie, cut to the chase," she says. Denise rolls her eyes in uncanny Keaton style and begins:

"About 15 years ago, I was a twenty-two-year-old cadet, and it was only my second time at sea. The first day on the ship, I was standing by the gangway next to this huge wiper named Ben. He said to me in a friendly way, 'You goin' ashore tonight, Denise?' 'No, I don't think so, Ben.' 'Well this may be your last chance to get some action. Have you ever tried it with a woman? My girlfriend's picking me up, and I could watch you two gettin' it on.' I knew this was only the beginning of a three-month voyage together, so I stayed stony-faced and repeated, 'Uh, no, Ben . . . I think I'll just stay aboard.'

"The whole voyage Ben stalked me from the shadows. But I finally got him. Bunkering on a drizzly cold night in Livorno, Italy, Ben suddenly appeared next to me and whispered, 'Hey, Denise, you've been seventy-five days out here without sex . . . don't you like men?' I smiled sweetly and waved my right hand at him. 'Ben, meet Rightie — hasn't failed me yet.' That was a first: Ben speechless.

"Then there was the electrician — a madman with crazy wild eyes. He kept watching me too: I'd be walking along the deck and he'd pop out of the doorway like a weasel. I could read his mind: 'Where's she been? Where's she going?'

"Now to the really bad part. There were only three of us working the engine room — the other two being a nice Third Assistant, John, and the First Engineer. The First was not only a dictator, but he was mean. Like, I knew what size wrench to pick because I'd always messed around with cars, but he would always say he'd ordered a different one and then get furious at me. The Third took a lot of the grief and was a buffer between us. But then the First was banging on a fitting which John was holding; his hammer missed and broke my buddy's arm in two places. So he had to fly home. The next six weeks alone in the engine room with the First were bloody hell.

"Meanwhile, we'd docked at Takandi on the Ivory Coast. Some of the guys had spent the whole trip over bad-mouthing blacks, then tramped off to the cathouse with the native whores. Even the married guys couldn't get there fast enough.

"The Captain always hung out in his room; so did the Chief Engineer who was drying out. I thought maybe I'd found a friend in the Second Assistant Engineer, who showed me pictures of his wife and kids and was very helpful. Wrong. I found out that another female cadet had been on the ship the year before. She took up with the "nice" married Second, and the electrician went nuts because he wasn't 'picked'. He wrote both her academy and the Coast Guard to complain. So that was the hidden agenda on board: the men were jockeying around to get the prize, and this time The Prize was me!"

"Wow, Denise," I comment, "You must be pretty tough to have stayed in the business."

"You don't know the half of it. Two weeks after that fateful voyage, I was on another ship. The Chief Engineer who signed me on was classic Kings Point: shiny shoes and slicked-back hair. I was just starting to feel at ease when he offered, 'I know you have to work on your sea project and the books are right here in my office — so come in any time.' He sounded so oily, I ran down the hall and locked myself in my room. But eventually I found two crewmen on that ship I could trust: an older First (who suggested we change seats in the mess so the Chief couldn't stare at me) and the ultimate comrade: the Second — who was gay."

"So eventually, did these experiences make you stronger?" I press on.

"I wish I could say so. What they actually did was some permanent damage. I never felt the same way about seamen, or even men in general, again. When I got home after that second trip, I even looked at my Dad in a different light: what would he do, how would he be, if you put him on a ship?"

Jess chimes in, "Do you remember, Dennie, that I sailed with a First like yours at the same time my ex-husband was drinking and putting me down? Yes, "damage" is the only way to describe it."

Denise grins. "But sometimes, we have our little victories. My first year of engineering school, I was the only female in a class of forty. A guy came up to me the second day, he was tough ex-Navy, tattoos and all, and asked what I was doing there. 'Excuse me? I'm here to study and get my degree.' 'Well you're taking space away from the white male . . . it seems he doesn't have any rights anymore . . . you should just go home.' I shrugged, said 'I'm sorry you feel that way,' and walked away. I was first in my class that year and stayed in the top three. Before we graduated, he admitted, 'I was wrong; I'd choose you as my shipmate any day.'

"But there's a bizarre end to these stories. A couple of years later my old friend John, the Third Engineer, phoned, 'Wait till you hear this! Our favorite First Engineer was just bludgeoned to death by a wiper. The wiper was so enraged by the guy's meanness, he didn't even bother to dump the evidence overboard.' "

So here they are: two survivors of twenty years in a tough, dangerous man's world. I admire their grit and dedication. I leave them with, "I hope what you've done will help the new women joining the Merchant Marine."

"Don't hold your breath!" they yell in unison.

I find Bob in our room, laying out a civilian shirt on the bed. "I forgot to tell you . . . a night mate comes aboard in Long Beach. He takes over my watch, which means we can finally sleep all night. I'll be able to leave the ship around supper time, so how would you like a real date tonight? On the Queen Mary?" *I blurt out, "Gee, Honey, I thought you'd never ask."*

I drag the duffel bag from the back of the closet and take out the one pair of decent pants I'd put in six weeks ago. I'd neglected to include a blouse, so one of the well-worn turtlenecks will have to do. I smile as I assemble my "outfit," recalling photos from the glory days of the Queen *and other luxury liners. Steamer trunks of clothes to change several times a day: for sports on the promenade deck, for lunch and high tea, for a glittering evening with music and five-course meals and French wines. But I will take whatever crumb I can nibble.*

By the time the Chief Mate has satisfied the Coast Guard brass, delivered all his documents to the right departments, rounded up the stragglers who had no urgency about signing on, given the night mate instructions about the cargo and passed over the precious reefer book, it's after 1700. I'm hungry, my appetite having adjusted itself to the five o'clock shipboard feeding. I ask Bob, "What do you think about having dinner on board? Then we could do dessert on the Queen?" *I have a hidden agenda besides hunger: I'd never had Filipino food, and the new cook had promised a treat, hadn't he?*

Jake's tongue-tingling, lip-smacking entree is a hit, reminding us of how deprived we've been with Louis' menus. Chicken, falling off the bone, swims in a tangy sauerbraten-like sauce. When I go back for seconds, I plead for the recipe. Jake is pleased, "My dad was a pretty famous Steward out here. It's his Chicken Adobo:

> 1 chicken, cut up
> 2 cups cider vinegar
> ½ cup soy sauce
> ¼ cup pineapple juice
> 6 corn peppers (or other hot peppers)
> 4 cloves garlic
> 2 bay leaves

Mix and marinate everything for a few hours or overnight, then simmer on very low heat for several hours. Serve over rice. Best to make a big batch of it — it gets better each time you heat it up."

I thought that Bob might spring for a taxi on this special occasion, but no, it's back on the bikes. By now, my built-up legs pump straight and smooth, and my hands grip the handlebars with confidence. Though the Queen Mary appears to be a short ride from Endurance, security gates and chain-link fences and other docks create many mazes. Fortunately, there is very little night-time traffic around the port area as we pedal on commercial avenues and overpasses, even onto a highway. But the liner, aglow with lights and looming large, eludes us.

Frustrated, Bob growls, "Look, I'm tired of this — let's head straight for the damn thing. Are you up for walking the bikes down these embankments?" I hope the old Queen is worth it as we set off down a 45° slope, through two gnarly knolls bisected by another road. Royal Queen Mary must be stirring in her grave as I make my grand entrance aboard her namesake, leaves in my hair, burrs on my pants and mud-soaked boots.

But the ship is still magnificent, all twelve decks and twenty-one elevators. After I clean up in an authentically retro bathroom, we take a self-guided tour around the Promenade Deck. Full-size photographs of celebrities, whose feet had preceded us on the same polished path, are on the walls. Clark Gable flashes his famous dimples, and Marlene Dietrich poses in a long coat, dense with sacrificial minks.

Since I'd promised Bob dessert (before the double portion of chicken, alas), we find an elegant restaurant. Our window table overlooks the lights of Long Beach, which reflect off the still water. Despite my steerage appearance, I feel like a first-class passenger. The white linen tablecloth shows no signs of elbow grease; crystal salt and pepper shakers have replaced the plastic condiment caddy on Endurance; and a French waitress in a classic black and white uniform hovers near us, eager to suggest and serve.

We gorge ourselves on her recommendation: Long Beach Sundaes — brandy snifters packed with high-butterfat ice cream, layers of strawberries, and rivulets of chocolate sauce, capped with a dome of whipped cream and a fistful of pecans. In this bewitching setting, to me the sundae surpasses the Coquilles St. Jacques and Biftek au Poivre formerly served aboard.

We stroll to the Observation Lounge, a semi-circular room that resides, appropriately, underneath the wheelhouse. No one, wisely, has meddled with the curvilinear bar, fluted columns and inlaid woods that spell high Art Deco. As Bob whirls me in a dance around the otherwise-empty parquet floor, I hang on tight, dizzy with his arms holding me, plus high blood sugar and too much wine. Aboard a now land-locked shrine to romance and glamour, I time-travel back to an era as exotic as the Far East.

I fall into bed with my head still spinning. Containers crash down, just like on my first night aboard, but this time I fall asleep immediately and deeply. "A sailor can sleep anywhere," the saying goes.

Chapter 23

JANUARY 6

Somehow I'd forgotten that the alarm was set for 0600 — wishful think-
ing, I guess, that our next-to-last day together might start with love in the
morning. For after we'd sailed up the coast to Oakland, I would have to get
off. Sea-Land's policy limits the Spouse to one voyage in a calendar year.
But Bob is gone and only returns to get me for breakfast. The tension in his
face breaks my reverie about togetherness aboard the Queen. *"Is it worse*
today than usual?" I sympathize.

"Just the same old you-know-what," he answers. "I always have a
headache on departure day from Long Beach. Getting the ship out on time is
like conducting. All the musicians must finish on the same note. The
longshoremen can screw up without consequence, but if a Chief Mate
delays a sailing, he's in danger of getting fired. If there's one thing the
company can't tolerate, it's a ship leaving late.

"What's really hard," he says, pocketing the aspirin bottle, "is knowing
I'm going back out to do this all over again. I just want to go home with
you . . ." Reluctant to show more emotion, he turns away.

At breakfast, the Chief Mate was up/down/back/forth like a
wind-up toy as he gave the Bosun instructions about jury-

rigging the lifeboat wires. The wrong ones had been delivered. He instructed the cadet to stow the medications, which had finally arrived. He rounded up one of the new ABs with big muscles and explained, "We need a strong arm to free up the stacking frame in #4 hatch. The company keeps pestering us to paint the twistlocks yellow, to help the crane operators get their bearings, but the paint got in between the peckerheads, freezing the locking mechanisms."

By some Act of Providence, the Second Mate noticed that the ship was down at the head. It's an old superstition — never proven — that this makes the wheel unresponsive. There was a mad rush to trim the ship: the C/M rang the engine room and ordered immediate deballasting of the forward tank. All seven hundred tons. By sailing time minus three hours, the final cargo plan still hadn't been delivered, and the C/M had to ask the Captain to call the Marine Office.

Finally, when the Chief Mate checked the container securing, he had to fix a couple of unsecured ones himself. He commented, "All the cargo will be double-checked again before we head out from Oakland. I'm always thinking worst-case scenario."

Let me out of here. In the distance, the skyscrapers of Long Beach, like a group of distinguished guests at a party, beckon me. I step around the mountains of dirty laundry waiting to be offloaded, and onto the Sea-Land shuttle bus. After the security gate, I walk alongside a phalanx of trucks lined up to take our cargo, and down to a Port Authority building where The City of Long Beach kindly provides a free bus to downtown.

I've been dropped back into Civilization. The bus and the streets are clean, immaculate really, around a new convention center. All the signs are in English. The atmosphere is clear as Windexed glass. No surgical masks or kamikaze motorbikes. No piles of rubble, squatting on sidewalks, or snake soup. It's all so agreeable, so American, but strangely, a little boring. I'm able to get a haircut, buy the New York Times, a rosy lipstick, and a bottle of Napa Valley merlot. But once the necessities are out of the way, Endurance pulls me back. I'm in plenty of time for cast-off.

I open the merlot and pour it to the top of a juice glass I'd stolen from the galley. When I look out the porthole, I remember Bob's orchestra metaphor about everything coming together at once. As the last truck drives off, diesel smoke is already shooting up from Endurance's two tugboats. The fore and aft lines are cast off from shore and reeled aboard the ship. M/V Endurance is bound for sea once more.

As we glide out to the channel, I look back toward the Queen Mary. From a different angle and a new perspective, the Sea-Land terminal stands between us and her; and slowly her hull disappears behind a mountain of containers until all I can see is her superstructure and smokestacks. The poor old Queen: even with her endearing beauty, as a sea creature, she's functionally obsolete. Instead of pampered human passengers, chemicals, "chicken paws" and plastic casters sail the oceans now.

I wonder again how many more years Endurance has left under her keel. Sea-Land is already anticipating the decline of the D-9's, like the C-4's before them, by ordering a new generation of containerships: longer, faster, designed to carry larger boxes. And if Endurance is able to survive another fifteen years or so, what flag will flutter from her stern pole?

My emotions run as strong as the tide that thrusts us through the Santa Barbara Channel:

I feel sad for all the scrapped, mothballed or permanently tethered vessels, each of which was once a "she" with a real identity and purpose.

I'm proud. Of the M/V Endurance which, true to her name, has once again delivered, in spite of icy winds, menacing seas and human discord.

Of her officers and crew who, shorthanded, weary, deprived, still band together to keep U.S. commerce rolling. And of Sea-Land; it invented a better way to transport cargo and its vessels still ply the coasts and circle the globe. Whatever happens to American shipping in the future, Sea-Land has had an impressive past.

I'm grateful that I was able to step inside a working ship and explore her from stem to stern, engine room to bridge. Though I entered the world of merchant shipping unbaptized like Dana, I'm leaving it with respect for those who make their living battling the sea.

Like my hero, I will walk down the gangway to resume a landlubber's life. And like him, "I bade farewell — yes, I do not doubt forever — to those scenes which, however changed or unchanged, must always possess an ineffable interest for me." A ship's lighted bridge will always make me wonder, and remember. I know I can always return in my mind to that place where sky and water meet.

ADDENDUM TO THE STORY OF KOBE

At 5:46 A.M., on January 17, 1995, the Great Hanshin Earthquake struck Kobe. It killed more than 6,300, injured 35,000 and left more than 300,000 homeless. Very few residents had earthquake insurance, which is prohibitively expensive in Japan.

Most of the new Rokko Island buildings withstood the quake and there were no fatalities among Sea-Land people, although many lost their homes. The inside of the container terminal caved in and the cranes buckled. Within six months the automatic cranes were back in service. Sea-Land is still calling at Kobe.

ADDENDUM TO THE PROBLEM OF FOREIGN FLAGGING

On Oct. 8, 1996, President Clinton signed into law HR 1350, the "Maritime Security Act of 1995." The new ten year ship subsidy program will provide $100 million annually to keep approximately fifty American vessels and their American citizen crews under the U.S. flag. The operator of each ship will receive $2.1 million a year in exchange for making the vessel *and* its intermodal network available to the Defense Department when needed. *Endurance* is one of the chosen ships.

In supporting the bill, Senator Barbara Mikulski told the Senate: "History has taught us one thing: we cannot rely on foreign countries with foreign crews to transport our military cargo in time of war. . . . When the world makes a 911 call to America, we must be ready." And President Clinton announced when he signed the bill, "This Act sets the course for America's Merchant Marine into the twenty-first century. The American flag must always sail in the sea lanes of the world. . . ."

ADDENDA TO MAJOR U.S. SHIPPING LINES

Lykes Lines, one of the four major U.S. international shipping lines, has operated under Chapter 11 of the U.S. federal bankruptcy code since October 1995. As part of the reorganization plan, Canadian Pacific Ltd. was scheduled to acquire the services of Lykes Lines, the U.S. container shipping operation of Lykes Brothers Steamship Co., as this book went to press.

In April 1997, Neptune Orient Lines, a Singapore company, agreed to acquire APL, the former American President Lines, another of the four major U.S. international shipping lines. According to the *New York Times*, "The deal is subject to approval by the United States Department of Transportation. The Defense Department has already been notified." To retain APL's business of shipping supplies for the Pentago, APL's ships will continue to sail under the American flag and will retain the APL name, an APL executive said.

Glossary

AB. Able-bodied seaman.

aft (or after). Toward, near, or at the stern of a vessel.

barograph. A recording barometer.

Beaufort Scale. A numerical scale for indicating wind speed, devised by an Admiral named Beaufort in 1805:

Beaufort Force #	State of Air	Wind Velocity in Knots
0	calm	0–1
1	light airs	1–3
2	slight breeze	4–6
3	gentle breeze	7–10
4	moderate breeze	11–16
5	fresh breeze	17–21
6	strong breeze	22–27
7	moderate gale	28–33
8	fresh gale	34–40
9	strong gale	41–47
10	whole gale	48–55
11	storm	56–65
12	hurricane	above 65

bitt. A strong post projecting above the deck of a ship, used for securing cables, lines for towing, etc.

bollard. A post firmly secured to a wharf, etc., for mooring vessels by means of lines extending from the vessel and secured to the post.

bosun (also "bo's'n"; a contraction of its original form "boat-swain"). An unlicensed deck officer on a merchant vessel, in charge of rigging, anchors, cables, etc.

bow. The forward part of a ship.

bowline. A knot tied in such a way that a loop is made at the end of the rope; it will not slip or jam.

bridge. The control station of a vessel.

brig. A two-masted square-rigged vessel, also a place of confinement or detention, especially in the U.S. Navy or Marines.

Bristol fashion. Shipshape; clean, neat, orderly, and conforming to high standards of seamanship.

bulkhead. Any of various wall-like divisions between compartments inside a vessel for forming watertight compartments, subdividing space, strengthening the structure, preventing surge of liquids, etc.

bunker. To provide fuel for a vessel. Bunkers — the oil being received during bunkering.

carling. A short fore-and-aft beam running beside a hatchway, mast hole, or other deck opening.

Charts. Seagoing maps.

China Coaster. A seaman who's obsessed with Oriental culture and women. Up until the 1960s, an American pension could provide a luxurious lifestyle in the Far East.

davits. Small cast-iron cranes, fitted with hoisting and lowering gear, from which lifeboats are slung.

dogs. Metal hand clips on doors, hatch covers or portholes, which when turned, force a rubber gasket tight to ensure a waterproof seal.

draft. The depth to which a vessel is submerged.

EPIRB (Emergency Position Indicating Radiobeacon). A device that transmits a distinctive tone signal on two aircraft frequencies. This signal first alerts passing aircraft that an emergency exists and later guides searchers to the scene.

ETA. Estimated time of arrival.

fathometer. A device to measure the depth of water underneath a ship's keel.

fix. A ship's position obtained from observations of landmarks or sea-marks or by astronomical, radio, or electronic means of navigation.

forecastle (also fo'c'sle). A superstructure at or immediately aft of the bow of a vessel, used as a shelter for stores, machinery, etc., or as quarters for seamen.

gantry. Any of various spanning frameworks, as a bridgelike portion of certain cranes.

gimbals. A device for supporting anything (such as a magnetic compass) in such a manner that it will remain essentially horizontal when the support tilts.

GPS. Global Positioning Satellite.

great circle sailing. A method of navigating a ship along the shortest distance between the point of departure and the point of arrival.

hasp. A clasp on a door or lid, etc., especially one passing over a staple and fastened by a pin or padlock.

hawsepipe. The inclined pipe or tube near the bow that leads from the *hawsehole* (a hole in the deck) of a ship, to an opening on the side of the vessel.

head. Toilet; lavatory.

heel. To tip or lean to one side (either from an uneven distribution of weight or the force of the wind).

hold. A large compartment below decks, used mainly for the stowage of cargo.

hooker. An old-fashioned or clumsy vessel.

hull. The main body of a ship (main deck, sides, and bottom).

intermodal shipping. An integrated transportation system that coordinates the water, rail and/or truck movement of containerized cargo under a single carrier's control in a continuous movement from shipper to consignee.

international dateline. A theoretical line at the 180° meridian; areas to the east of it are a calendar day earlier than areas to the west.

Jacob's ladder. A rope ladder, lowered from the deck, as when pilots or passengers come aboard.

keelhauling. A naval punishment introduced in the fifteenth century. The offender was tied to a rope and hauled beneath the keel of the ship, from one side to the other.

latitude. One of the co-ordinates used to describe a position on the earth's surface: north or south of the equator. Before satellite navigation, mariners calculated latitude by measuring the midday altitude of the sun.

lee. Protecting shelter; the side of a ship that is sheltered from the wind.

lighter. A vessel without power, towed by tugs, used to haul cargo from ship to shore or shore to ship.

list. Continuous inclination of a ship to one side.

longitude. *See* **meridian**.

longshoreman. In the past when ships were unloaded the sailors passed the goods from the ships to men 'along' the shore — and so they were called "long-shore-men. Today, longshoremen load and unload ships.

manrope. A rope placed at the side of a gangway, ladder, etc., to serve as a steadying line (especially when disembarking a pilot).

master. In current usage, one who commands a merchant vessel; captain.

merchant marine. The vessels of a nation that are engaged in commerce; the officers and crews of such vessels.

meridian (also known as a line of longitude). It describes the position east or west of the prime meridian: a north-south great circle line running through Greenwich, England. It used to be calculated by an accurate clock (called a *chronometer*), comparing Greenwich time with local time.

mess. The place on a ship where group meals are taken.

oakum. Loosely twisted hemp or jute fiber impregnated with tar and used in caulking seams (as in wooden ships).

on the beach. Ashore.

packet. A boat that carries mail, passengers, and goods regularly on a fixed route.

pitch. The alternate rise and fall of the bow of a vessel proceeding through waves.

poop. A short raised deck at the after end of a ship.

quartermaster. In merchant vessels, an able seaman who steers and keeps the bridge and its equipment clean; he assists in navigation.

roll. The alternating motion of a boat to port and starboard (about its fore-and-aft axis).

St. Elmo's fire. A fiery electrical discharge, usually seen around mastheads and yardarms of ships and church spires.

scuttlebutt. Gossip, rumors, so called because sailors used to gather around the scuttle butt, a cask for drinking water.

slop chest. A supply of clothing, tobacco, and other personal goods for sale to seamen during a voyage; (formerly) a chest containing this supply.

stern. The after portion of a boat.

supernumerary. Being in excess of the usual, proper, or prescribed number; extra; superfluous.

trough. The depression in the water between two waves.

twistlocks. Fist-sized fittings that join and secure corners of containers loaded one above the other.

wake. The track in the water of a moving vessel.

Bibliography

The Aleutians Campaign, June 1942—August 1943. Publications Branch, Office of Naval Intelligence, United States Navy, 1945.

Bowditch, Nathaniel, *American Practical Navigator.* Defense Mapping Agency Hydrographic Center, 1977.

Brown, Capt. Edwin Peter, *In the Wake of Whales.* Old Orient Press, 1988.

Buckley, Christopher, *Steaming to Bamboola.* Penguin Books, 1987.

Dana, Richard Henry, *Two Years Before the Mast.* Penguin Books, 1964.

Gillmer, Thomas C., *Working Watercraft.* International Marine Publishing Company, 1972.

Facts About Korea. Korean Overseas Information Service, 1993.

Hayler, William B., ed., *Merchant Marine Officers' Handbook.* Cornell Maritime Press, 1989.

Hoehling, A. A., *Ships That Changed History.* Madison Books, 1992.

Kemp, Peter, ed., *The Oxford Companion to Ships & The Sea.* Oxford University Press, 1976.

Laing, Alexander, *American Ships.* American Heritage Press, 1971.

London, Jack, *The Sea-Wolf.* Penguin Books, 1964.

Marshall, Michael, *Ocean Traders.* Facts on File, 1990.

McPhee, John, *Looking for a Ship.* Macfarlane Walter & Ross, 1990.

Nakiel, Richard, and Antony Preston, *Atlas of Maritime History*. W. H. Smith Publishers Inc., 1987.

Paine, Ralph D., *The Old Merchant Marine*. Yale University Press, 1919.

Rath, Eric, *Container Systems*. John Wiley & Sons, 1984.

Ritter, Harry, *Alaska's History*. Alaska Northwest Books, 1993.

Rowen, Roy, *The Four Days of* Mayaguez. W. W. Norton & Company, 1975.

Spectre, Peter H., *The Mariner's Book of Days*. WoodenBoat Books, 1994.

Storey, Robert, *Hong Kong, Macau & Canton — A Travel Survival Kit*, 2nd ed. Australia: Lonely Planet Publications, 1992.

Transportation Research Board, *Intermodal Marine Container Transportation*. National Research Council, 1992.

Villiers, Alan, *Of Ships and Men*. Arco Publishing Co., 1964.

U.S. Department of Commerce/Maritime Administration, *The United States Merchant Marine — A Brief History*. 1950.

Newsletters

Insight (Sea-Land Service, Inc.)

The Master, Mate & Pilot (International Organization of Masters, Mates & Pilots)